Journey through

Far and beyond t

adventures

By: Honeylet Nunez Orr

Table of Contents

Chapter 1

Introduction

My first book, which I hope you have read, was all about my journey through adversities, far and beyond the life and adventures in the Philippines, and this book will continue my journey in the United Kingdom. I would be delighted to take you back to the time when it all started, and I can promise that as you read this book, you will experience the essence of my life in the United Kingdom when I recount my hopes, dreams, aspirations, tribulations, and successes. I hope my book will inspire new generations as they start their life journeys and that even though life is full of adventures and adversities, through God's will there is light at the end of the tunnel. Endurance, pain, and suffering through oppression and racism will never succeed as love and justice will conquer everything through Christ the saviour. Happiness and contentment will be for evermore the greatest achievements of all.

I finished my first book at the point of leaving my family in the Philippines for the first time in my life to start my nursing career in the United Kingdom.

Before leaving I visited all my relatives in the Philippines to say goodbye, which was greatly appreciated. They wished me luck and offered prayers and love as I started my journey. It was difficult to digest the fact that I was leaving my home for the first time, and that I was uncertain of what challenges I would face in the United Kingdom.

I left home with mixed feelings. On the one hand, I was excited to be able to fulfil my dreams of working abroad as a nurse and earning money to help my family and relatives. On the other hand, I was sad to leave my family behind for the first time since I was born. Was it to be a goodbye? Would I ever see them again?

At the airport, I said goodbye to every one of my family. As I went through the departure gates, courage deserted me and tears dropped down my cheeks as I waved goodbye, and all shadows of my family's presence were lost. I faced a new prospect for my next journey through adversities, far away in the United Kingdom.

Chapter 2

Arrival in the United Kingdom

Bon Voyage

The Philippines airport was full of people. I could not help observing the reaction of those around me as they left the Philippines leaving behind their loved ones. I do not know why I should have cared and bothered to scrutinise the emotions of the people around me, but it was essential for me at that time. I was not trying to compare their behaviour with mine, but I was just curious to observe their genuine emotions. Whatever, I came to the conclusion that people react differently in certain situations.

At the airport, I observed a mixture of feelings of sadness, joy, anxiety, despair, and loss. There were some happy people, who I thought were only visiting the Philippines and were now going back to their families on the other side of the world. How could they be so joyful if that was not the case? On the other hand, there were sad faces of people like me, who may also have been saying goodbye to loved ones. I could never know their true emotional state, but I assumed that leaving loved ones behind was an extremely emotional experience. How could that be joy? You may remember from my last book that life can be too short, and one never knows when your time of death will occur. Therefore, express love, do something worthwhile in the world before it is too late: saying goodbye and sending prayers and best wishes were amazing leaving presents for someone.

The airport screening protocols were at their strictest. My relatives told me to expect this, but I was not prepared to experience what I did. Knowledge is one thing, experience another. I had to ensure I had the correct identification (my passport), the correct visa, and the correct boarding pass. My physical appearance had to match these documents, otherwise I could be accused of fraud. The next hurdle was to check that my baggage was the correct weight to pass on to the baggage conveyor belt. This was also screened for illegal drugs or any suspicious terrorist materials. What a system! But, looking back, I can understand that it was necessary for the safety of passengers.

When I was boarding the plane I met my nursing group hired at the same time as me to work in the United Kingdom. I remember the names of Rose, Ofel, Rowena, Arnel, Christine, Annie, Nita, and Ronald. We were a group of nurses boarded on an Air France plane for the United Kingdom via France. Including the transfer in France, the journey time was 20–24 hours. We departed on 29 April but landed in the United Kingdom on the same date due to the time difference.

Due to my naivety and inexperience I was anxious about plane travel. I had heard stories of plane crashes in the past and could not help myself thinking about dying in a plane crash. It was a remarkable experience for me, aged 24, as this was the first time I had ever travelled by boat or plane. Turbulence made me anxious, and prayer was the only way to give me peace of mind, as it had done in times of trouble in the past. I was even able to sleep on the flight.

I finally reached my ultimate destination of the United Kingdom, the land which was meant to fulfil my dreams and aspirations in life, the land of endless opportunities for a better future. I was tired but excited about my new prospects and was very thankful to God that my journey was safe and a great experience after all. When we arrived, I and the other nurses collected our baggage from the conveyor belt.

On arrival in the United Kingdom, the airport was full of people from many different backgrounds. I had never seen such a diverse crowd except for in movies or on television. But this was real: I was in a foreign land with people of different backgrounds around me — white, black, Asians, small, tall, all speaking different languages. It was an amazing scene: a foreign land in which I would be working with people like these. I am not sure how I felt at the time; I was full of emotion and tiredness made comprehension difficult. However, I am certain I knew I had something to look forward to — an adventure, the challenge of a lifetime — and that I had the faith and courage to succeed and thrive.

I was ushered along with my group of nurses, who seemed to know what to do as some of them had worked abroad in the Middle East. At immigration, our passports and visas were checked and, at long last, we entered the United Kingdom. We were advised to look for a placard for 'Royal Free Hospital' on exiting the airport as the driver would take us to our accommodation. The weather was cloudy and windy, strikingly different from the Philippines, and the damp air made me feel colder than it actually was. We soon found our driver, and the small coach took us to Coppets Wood Accommodation, Muswell Hill, London where we were going to stay.

Coppets Wood Accommodation

You can imagine how cold I felt when we reached the accommodation as it was dark and gloomy at the time of our arrival. As soon as we reached our destination, we received a welcome greeting from everyone already living there. I was very thankful for this friendly gesture for us newcomers. It gave us reassurance of support from the community around us, a welcome gift from God.

Coppets Wood Accommodation was a hospital that had been converted to nurses' accommodation. In the past it had dealt in communicable diseases. The accommodation therefore consisted of single bedrooms each with its own washing basin. Although it was a hospital in the past, it seemed a great idea to transform it to accommodation. As a nurses' home, it had become accepted as part of the local community.

We were shown around the shared facilities of the accommodation — the kitchens, toilets, bathrooms, and living room. However, our own bedrooms were considered our own private space. My bedroom had a single bed, a study table, chair, small drawer, one basin and tap. In addition, it benefitted from a huge window overlooking the main road allowing lots of sunlight to brighten the room. I was also extremely grateful that I was closer to the rooms of my group of nurses, who provided God-given help in times of need.

The Royal Free Hospital gave us a few days to settle and adjust to our new environment before we started our orientation programme. In addition, this was an opportunity for us to buy food and any necessary basic equipment, which we did in nearby shops on the following day. We were shown around by a nice kind-hearted man called Herman.

I remember the very first day we were taken out from our accommodation: it was gloomy, dark, and cold, and the road was completely silent. I hardly saw anyone around. The place seemed deserted, very different from the Philippines that I grew up in. Herman took us to the local Tesco to buy food. I bought a small bag of rice, the basic carbohydrate I ate three times a day in the Philippines. I was surprised to have to buy a small bag as I was used to having a 50 kg sack stocked in our home in the Philippines.

The miracle was that I was able to buy all the basics with the small allowance I was given. With the money I had, I successfully provided myself with sardines, bread, milk, rice, noodles, eggs etc. In addition, I bought an international phone card that I used to call the Philippines as soon as I got home from shopping. You will never know how delighted I was to hear the voices of my family; and my family was really glad that my journey had gone well, and that I was safe and sound. It was an emotional call: they missed me as I missed them.

Back then, we did not have the technology we have now as I am writing this book. At the time, I needed a mobile phone and an international phone card to dial the Philippines, and I had to pay for the use of both. I needed to dial the number on the phone card, enter the PIN number, and then the country code and the number in the Philippines. It was a tedious process, and the worst thing was always being cut off in the middle of the conversation. It could take at least twice or three times longer than usual. Moreover, the international card was not cheap: it could sometimes cost £10 for a 30-minute conversation. I was therefore grateful for WhatsApp and Messenger that now allow international calls to be made for free. They really help to communicate, wherever you are in the world.

One of the good things at Coppets Wood was the group of friends who were willing to show us around London and get us started with the things that we needed. Herman once again volunteered to show us around as a group; he taught us to buy train tickets and to read an underground map. He took us to famous tourist attractions such Westminster Abbey, Westminster Cathedral, the Houses of Parliament, London Eye, Chinatown, Leicester Square, Buckingham Palace, and Piccadilly Circus. It was a fascinating tour to see wonderfully crafted buildings with great histories, and such a delight to have seen so many wonders the world has to offer.

My group of nurses was later to become my friends, and some, who were older than me, I treated as my elder brothers and sisters. It was such a great joy to share my passion and excitement with them as we all ventured together on this new opportunity.

Meeting up with old friends in the UK

Not long after I arrived at Coppets Wood, my friend Irwin visited me. The meeting had been arranged before I left the Philippines. Irwin was one of my best friends in the College of Nursing, and he came to the UK a few months before me. He was working at King's Lynn Hospital in Norfolk as a staff nurse in one of the medical and surgical wards. It was so nice to see an old friend in the UK. On his visits he updated me with what had been happening in his life. He seemed to be having a great time and he never told me of any negative experiences.

Another friend of mine also came to visit me, unexpectedly. I was surprised, as he did not have my UK contact details. His name was Alwyn, an Irishman I met doing voluntary work in 1999 at the Jimmy Carter housing project in the Philippines. Irwin was also there when Alwyn visited me and I introduced them to each other.

Irwin showed me around London and then went back to the countryside where he was working. I had to ring him a couple of times when I needed support, for which I was grateful, as at least I had a friend here from back home. In addition, Alwyn volunteered to be my tourist guide once a week, which was a bonus as he knew London very well from working and living there. He never failed to keep his word to show me around and

I commended him for his generosity, kindness, and word of honour. He was a truly remarkable individual.

Another friend of mine called Armie later came to the United Kingdom. She was a colleague in the Chinese General Hospital. She was assigned to work in one of the biggest hospitals in Birmingham as a staff nurse in the medical and surgical ward. She was a delightful, trusted, and loyal friend who was always there for support in times of need: a really kind and genuinely amazing individual. We came to see each other every now and then when she came to the United Kingdom. It was great to have this friend with me, such a great gift from God.

Pictures of my friends and myself in the United Kingdom

St Mary's Accommodation

St Mary's Accommodation was another nurses' accommodation of the Royal Free Hospital, located at the top of Hampstead Heath. In the past, this had been part of the Royal Free, but was later converted to accommodation. Compared to Coppets Wood, it had the advantage of being within walking distance of the hospital, so no public transport was required. As such, there was a long waiting list, which did not deter my friends and me in applying for this accommodation. Soon enough, we moved there, but I did not stay long as I moved to Golders Green, and I will explain why in the next chapter of my book.

Photo of my nursing group in the UK

Chapter 3

Royal Free Hospital

Orientation

The orientation was for new arrivals of nurses from the Philippines at the Royal Free Hospital. We had been provided with detailed information about the hospital facilities, education, and general patient services. Practical matters such as setting up bank accounts, National Insurance, and information on the Nursing and Midwifery Council (NMC) were also provided. After orientation, we were given the opportunity to be shown around the hospital and meet the staff working in the different areas. It was such an eventful day and a daunting experience, but the Royal Free Hospital gave us a great welcome. We then set up bank accounts in order to be paid our monthly salaries.

National Insurance is a government tax system and everyone over the age of 18 is issued a number. It is a compulsory requirement for anyone working in the UK so we dealt with this immediately. The NMC information reminded us that we must adhere to the code of conduct and behaviour as a nurse. NMC is a registered professional body for nursing, and we were required to be given this information as newcomers to the profession in the UK. The NMC was also there to help if any work-related issues arose. After the period of orientation, we were each dispatched to our contracted workplace.

Renal Transplant Ward

I was employed to work at the Royal Free's Renal Transplant Ward, located on the third floor of the hospital. My ward manager was Ann Mcreynolds, a genuinely supportive Irish lady who looked after me throughout my time working on her ward. She was a kind-hearted individual, compassionate, and who cared for my wellbeing. She showed great humility and I will never forget the kindness she showed me. The memories of the support she gave me were particularly important to someone like me who was new to nursing in the UK.

When I started on the ward I was assigned two senior nurses — Andreas from Sweden and Megan, an English nurse — who acted as mentors, teaching and guiding me through the various skills I needed on the ward. Before becoming a staff nurse I was required to become proficient in all the necessary nursing tasks and the mentoring formed part of the teaching structure of my six-month overseas nursing programme. My mentors were always approachable and helpful, although they were not always working with me.

The structure of nursing in the UK is completely different from that in the Philippines, which was based on American practice. In the Philippines, nursing was organised on functional lines in contrast to the holistic approach adopted in the UK. In the Philippines a charge nurse was responsible for carrying out doctors' orders and managing the ward. Each function, such as the monitoring and administration of intravenous fluids, observations, or basic needs like washing, were allocated to different nurses or healthcare workers.

In contrast, in the UK each nurse was allocated a certain number of patients and was responsible for carrying out all the functions necessary: providing medications, feeding, washing, observation and attending any imaging scans patients required. In theory, there was one healthcare assistant allocated per shift, but this was not always the case in practice. During my time on the ward I was allocated five or six patients to look after.

The work of a staff nurse was hard, requiring stamina, endurance, and physical resilience. I was on my feet all the time with little chance for breaks. I felt I did not have the time to attend to all the needs of my patients. I had to work overtime without pay in order to complete the nursing notes at the end of each shift as there was no time during the day to do this. It was tough for me as I always tried my best to give my patients excellent care and I felt frustrated that I was not able to perform at the highest standard due to lack of time. Without the strength and guidance from God I would not have been able to report for work as I was worried about making mistakes and being unable to fulfil my vocation of caring for my patients.

The classic case was if one or two of my patients became unwell during my shift, which meant that I had little time to spend on my other patients. One example of this was when one of my patients — a lovely middle-aged white man — became incontinent. On my day shift he was sleeping in his bed but later he developed diarrhoea which had spread all around his room. It was shocking to see him in such a devastating situation. What should I do as a nurse?

I could not help crying about my patient, who had no idea of what had happened and was confused. If there was a healthcare assistant that day, she was attending other patients. I had no choice, therefore, but to attend the patient myself. I took pleasure in giving him a proper shower, putting him in a new hospital gown to make him feel fresh, and helping the cleaner to clean the room. It was a great joy to see my patient well groomed, happy, and comfortable. I even gave him talcum powder to help him smell wonderfully. Unfortunately, however, later that day, he had diarrhoea twice again on my shift, and once more, I had no time to attend to my other patients.

In the Philippines, almost every patient has a relative at the bedside, often for twenty-four hours a day, and this was certainly the case in a private room of a private hospital. These relatives would take care of all the basic needs of the patient, such as feeding, drinking, turning, and washing. Therefore, the patient was not purely reliant on the nurses, giving them much more time to attend to other nursing duties.

In contrast, in the United Kingdom, visitors were only generally allowed during the visiting period. In most cases, there were no visits anyway, as relatives either lived far away or were too busy with their lives to visit regularly. Nurses were therefore responsible for all the patients' basic needs. As a staff nurse, I remember occasions when I had to attend a bell call from a patient five times in an hour just to give the patient a drink. This was fine, but it was difficult if I was attending an ill patient at the same time.

In my ward, we had two shifts per day — 8am to 8pm and 8pm to 8am — and these were rotated for all except the head nurse. In a week, there could be three to four night shifts followed by three to four day shifts, with some days off. During each twelve-hour shift, we were allowed a thirty-minute break without pay — either a morning, lunch, or afternoon tea on a day shift or a one-off break at night.

My first staff nurse uniform

My nurse uniform was also completely different from the Philippines. In the United Kingdom staff nurses wore a light blue tunic and no caps, while senior nurses wore a dark blue tunic. The structure of nursing was hierarchical with bands D, E, F, G, H, I etc. Nurses started at band D, the bottom of the ladder. To be promoted to a higher band you had to submit an application giving your job description, qualifications, and experience in order to be given the chance of an interview.

My ward specialised in renal patient care. There were a variety of patients. They could be pre- or post-transplant, and could have received transplants from either live or deceased donors. They could have had acute kidney disease in levels 2–3–4–5 categories; they could have had end-stage renal failure or be on renal replacement therapy for peritoneal, haemodialysis, or a failing transplant. Conditions included sepsis, uraemia, and suspected heart failure. There were two rooms allocated for haemodialysis, which were always occupied every shift. My mentor taught me how to operate a haemodialysis machine and perform dialysis on patients.

I was generally assigned to look after post-transplant patients, so I spent most of time observing and monitoring my patients. Post-transplant care was crucial to the success of the transplant, as every detail of observation, such as monitoring urine output, was important for the survival of the transplanted kidney. For example, a lower than expected urine output could mean blockage of the urinary system or be a sign of rejection which would require immediate medical intervention.

As I have previously remarked, working in the UK required a great deal of adjustment for me, due to the differences in structure and nursing practices, but I managed to successfully adapt. The most challenging and worst part of my experience was the inappropriate behaviour of some of my colleagues. I experienced a lack of support, compassion, and empathy. This was most noticeable when some colleagues were unable to understand my accent, which in turn intimidated me and made me feel like a nuisance. I felt that some of the staff were communicating unclearly on purpose in order to make it difficult for me to understand.

We spoke English as a second language and our teaching in schools and universities was in English too; therefore, we could communicate in English. However, we were generally slow to respond as we had to think beforehand. As a newcomer in this country, support should have been given in respect of this but, in my experience, the language problem was not taken into consideration. The staff and patients did not appreciate that their own accents were difficult for new foreign nurses to understand. I found the behaviour of the staff shocking and unprofessional and not in keeping with the NMC's code of conduct.

I even encountered racism from an unwell older white patient in the ward. It was hard to believe this attitude from an elderly sick patient. The incident occurred when he asked me for assistance for a 'number two'. I did not understand and asked him nicely what he meant but he just shouted at me that he needed a 'number two'. I felt confused and helpless, and in the end another member of staff helped him and explained to me what a 'number two' was.

I remember going home crying, and feeling lonely and sad most of the time. I did have friends but they were often busy. My family was far away and I had to deal with the situation on my own. Was it so hard to be kind and respectful to people? Why was there a need to be rude and harsh and to cause offence? Is humiliating someone acceptable? Am I not entitled to the same kind of treatment as anyone else? Was I treated differently because I came from the Philippines, a third-world foreign country? Was it because of my race? The experience left a scar that was difficult to forget. I had never experienced this in the Philippines, so it really upset me.

Reflecting on this experience, I strongly feel that additional support is required for new nurses coming to the UK from overseas. In addition, all staff should be educated in the cultural background of the foreign nurses in order to increase understanding. Moreover, mentoring is vitally important to the development of the beginner; mentors, therefore, should be given more time to teach, otherwise, they will not serve their purpose. Staff should behave professionally and always adhere to the NMC code of conduct. It is crucially important to adhere to the moral values of doing good, being kind and compassionate, and to love each other as Jesus taught us.

In addition, nurses from overseas should be given more education about what to expect when working in the UK. A more detailed education about the structure of the workforce and the nursing skills required would be useful, as would more exposure to the accents and the language. I appreciate, however, that such an exposure is only likely to happen when actually working overseas. Nevertheless, enhanced language skills would certainly be a benefit.

Falling in love

Falling in love is the most unforgettable memory I have. It was thrilling and exciting and I never imagined that I would fall in love again after my heart was broken years ago.

My love story began when I started meeting Alwyn once a week as he showed me around London. During these days, I got to know him very well and he was a great support while I was finding my feet at work and in life here in the UK. He is such a good, kind-hearted companion, a wise and helpful advisor who was available for me in times of need. He is a compassionate individual who patiently took time to understand me, and who spoke smoothly, clearly and with respect for someone like me. In him, I felt accepted as an individual who would be loved for the way I am.

Alwyn is a man of honour who always did as he promised. He is a wise, intelligent, sensible individual who always made our conversations interesting and fun. We enjoyed being in each other's company as it seemed we had much in common. It was such a treat to be collected from my accommodation each week and he always brought a homemade sandwich for us. We often had picnics in the parks in the sunshine. I always felt at ease in his presence and there seemed to be a great chemistry between us — a real gift of friendship.

One of the few meeting dates I had with Alwyn in London

I knew I had fallen in love with Alwyn but tried to stop myself due to the probable complications. Alwyn was about to leave the United Kingdom, so I tried to spend most of my free time with him up to when he had to say goodbye to me. It was a dreadful and painful day; I felt heartbroken once again, but had no choice but to let him go. I did not even go to the airport to see him off as it would have been too difficult for me. I consoled myself in the belief that things happen for a good reason and with God's will.

One day, however, not long after he had left, he phoned to say he was back to the United Kingdom in order to be with me. I was deeply touched, shocked, and became emotional as I never expected events to turn out this way. I prayed to God for guidance, and would accept whatever plan He had as He had never let me down in the past. I dated after my heart was broken in 1999 but I had not fallen in love with anyone until I met Alwyn. I knew my relationship with him was real and special, a love from a powerful and unexplained source. It produced sparks of wonderful emotions, a magnetic feeling that has never been erased from my memory.

Therefore, when he said that he had returned to the UK for me and wanted to be with me, my heart was full of gladness and joy. I felt slightly selfish as I wanted his love for myself; I felt we deserved each other. With him, I felt I was ready to settle down and to have a family; I wanted to do everything I could to be with him. I was being drawn down this path and could not explain the reason to myself. It was uncharacteristic of me to rush into a decision that would change my life forever. But I made the decision without hesitation, and with happiness, joy, and love.

To be honest, I had never imagined this was going to happen after such a short period of time in the UK. I was meant to concentrate on my career and make a living for my family, but it was by God's will that my life had taken an unexpected turn. I fully trusted Alwyn and God to lead me. I knew that it would be hard to explain this turn of events to my parents, who had different expectations, but also that they would understand my decision.

I was carried down this path of finding myself living with Alwyn, planning our family life, and discussing happy everlasting life together. I end this paragraph to say that love conquers everything, and that God will always be in control of

His plan for my life. I therefore had no fear as God has always been good to me since I was born into this life.

Northern Ireland

I met Alwyn's family — father, stepmother, brother, sister and her husband — for the first time in Bangor, Northern Ireland at Christmas 2001. I remember this as a pleasant visit, and that his family supported Alwyn and me. They were kind and accommodating; they accepted me and treated me with respect.

Bangor is a small town in County Down, a seaside tourist destination. It has an interesting mix of general clothing shops, bakeries, cafés, restaurants, pubs, and gift shops. The town is surrounded by country parks, beaches, seaside walks, and rivers and lakes, where ducks paddle. The parks are in areas of natural beauty, with gardens, trees, and flowers, whatever the season. The town itself has amazing libraries and swimming areas, and has easy access to other small towns nearby and Belfast. It caters for everyone: young, old, and families.

Alwyn's parents' house is located on the sea front overlooking the promenade, beach, Pickie Fun Park, water fountains, and the marina. Sitting in the front room of their house witnessing the beauty of God's creation was a delight: flocks of happy people on the promenade, joyful children playing in the fun park, water sparkling in the fountains, and the sunset at the end of the day. We normally walked along the sea front once a day, where I experienced the serenity of the seaside, the smell of the sea, and the invigorating wind on my face.

I found it pleasant walking along the sea front and hearing the powerful waves break on the rocks. Being surrounded by such natural beauty had a positive impact on my wellbeing. Moreover, the people we met would often stop and talk to us. I was struck by the feeling of community spirit in these encounters.

Bangor Promenade, Northern Ireland

However, on my visit to Northern Ireland I was struck by the lack of any coloured people. It may have been that my visit was short or that there were none living in this particular area. It was most noticeable when Alwyn and I met a toddler in Bangor Park when we were having our lunch break. The child could barely take her eyes off me. She seemed to find my face extraordinary. I could not help myself laughing and I asked her mother if I could take a photograph of me and her daughter as a souvenir of my visit to Northern Ireland.

The first encounter of a foreign person in Northern Ireland

It should not be forgotten that I visited Alwyn's family at Christmas and we all celebrated the day in Alwyn's sister's house. The whole family was served a sumptuous feast of turkey, gravy, roast potatoes, sprouts, carrots, and parsnips. We each had a Christmas cracker which we opened before the start of the meal and we wore the paper hats and read out the quiz in each of the crackers. After lunch we played board games and opened our Christmas presents. The day ended with Christmas pudding served with cream.

Christmas celebration

My overall experience was one of great fun, which was very different from London. Here, I found that I was accepted as a foreigner and I felt a great sense of community and an emphasis on family values.

First holiday back to the Philippines

In January 2002, I went back to the Philippines on holiday for the first time since I arrived in the UK. I cannot express the anticipation I felt, counting down the days before I would see my family again. I flew alone, although Alwyn joined me later and we flew back to the UK together. This was the first time my parents had met Alwyn so it was an exciting time for all of us.

It is traditional that overseas workers present gifts — called *pasalubong* — to their loved ones when they return home. In preparation, therefore, I had to buy presents for all my family and friends before the flight home. I busily rummaged around stores buying suitable presents such as dresses, shoes, perfumes, lotions, watches, wallets, and foods like chocolates. Gifts are traditional in Filipino culture and show appreciation as well as providing good luck to loved ones.

I felt obliged to follow in this tradition to show appreciation to my family for all the sacrifices they made in providing for me and educating me. It is the child's duty to pay their parents back for these sacrifices by giving them presents. It is also expected that you help your parents financially, and I never failed to send them a monthly allowance when I started working in the UK.

There are a lot of things my readers should know about Filipino culture. There is a craving for imported branded goods, and such cravings may be the result of poverty. It is generally felt that possessing branded goods makes one feel good about oneself, and being accepted and respected in society. Having a grand house, car or even a mobile phone, wearing branded clothes, jewellery, and expensive shoes, gets one noticed and can be pleasurable.

However, there is a downside. Some people almost kill themselves by working seven days a week in order to provide such luxurious benefits or expensive birthday parties for their loved ones. In my opinion, it is fine to spend money on luxury items if you have surplus cash, but if this is at the expense of your physical and mental health, then what is the point? Some people do find pleasure in giving expensive presents, but can you really be happy with the material things in life? Should you not aim to do good for others in order to enter eternal life in Heaven?

The answer has to depend on the individual as we all have the free will to lead the life we choose. We should, however, be mindful of what matters spiritually. In my opinion, happiness is an individual matter and depends on how one perceives life. I do hope for material success, but there are also many things that one cannot buy such as love, peace of mind, friendship, a family, good health, and being close to God. After years of nursing experience, I can share the story of one of my patients. She felt she had had a perfect life but then one day she woke up feeling unwell. Following tests in hospital, her diagnosis was bad and she could have died. This new reality completely changed her perspective on life for the better. But do you want to wait for bad things to happen before making changes? What happens to your earthly possessions when you die? Have they brought much to your life after all?

There is no harm in earning a living to provide the best for one's family and loved ones, but we should be aware of the evil effect of the excessive love of money as this can lead one astray and maybe destroy one's life. Moreover, we should be aware of the effects of a love of power as this can mean using one's authority to hurt people rather than treating them morally; in the case of sexual power, it could destroy your family. As God says, truth will come out in the end, and one should avoid being ashamed once the truth is finally revealed. Hiding the truth creates more problems than it solves and may mean having to commit a crime in order to do so, in which case there is no turning back. Human behaviour is complex and often difficult to understand and we are bound to make mistakes. In my case, I pray to God for guidance in order to avoid the temptation to commit a wrongdoing I will come to regret.

Anyway, the day came when I finally arrived in the Philippines and was grateful to God for bringing me safely home. I smelled the pollution as soon as the plane reached Manila and hope that politicians will one day find a solution to this. I was greeted by my family on exiting the airport, and can hardly explain the joy on their faces when we met. Their heartfelt love seemed magnified that day as they had been looking forward to seeing me for such a long time.

I spent most of my time visiting family and friends while I waited for Alwyn to arrive. One morning, however, I vomited as I was waiting to meet my friend Gina. Coincidentally, we had arranged to meet in one of the hospitals in Quezon City, Manila. My friend advised me to take a pregnancy test there, which turned out to be positive. This was confirmed by an intrauterine ultrasound scan performed by a gynaecological consultant.

I was shocked and happy with disbelief that I was pregnant for the first time. I could not have possibly imagined that I would discover this in the Philippines. Alwyn and I had been waiting for such news for a long time and it was unfortunate that it did not arrive sooner. However, once I received the confirmation

I passed it on to Alwyn immediately. He, too, was shocked to hear this wonderful news and could not wait to see me in the Philippines to celebrate this great blessing from God. A test of patience can sometimes be difficult, but the news arrived at the time according to God's will.

Thank you, Lord, for once again blessing Alwyn and me, as we finally start our family.

Visiting friends in the Philippines

First Pregnancy

Pregnancy was the most amazing and profound experience for me as part of motherhood. My moods were affected by the changing hormones in my body. It also led to physical changes as my body adapted to the growing foetus in my womb. I was tired all the time and was sometimes breathless as my lungs were compressed by the growing foetus.

However, although it may sound crazy, one of the advantages was the cessation of my monthly periods. I had cravings for particular foods while pregnant, and these cravings increased as the foetus continued to grow. I normally had well-cooked scrambled eggs with rice and a traditional Filipino homemade meal. All this food helped to support the growing foetus and the thought of a new-born baby was something I really looked forward to.

Part of the routine examinations while pregnant was abdominal doppler ultrasound, which is a thrilling experience for expectant parents. I made an appointment as an outpatient with the sonographer, who scanned my belly to confirm that the foetus was alive, was breathing, and had a beating heart. During the examination, the sonographer showed me the moving object on the screen; the movement and the sound of my baby's heart beating was the greatest experience in my life.

After the examination we were given a copy of the ultrasound picture of our baby. We were also offered the opportunity to learn our baby's gender, an offer we declined. Each couple must make their own decision about this; some may wish to know for personal or practical reasons, such as being better able to prepare for the birth. In contrast, Alwyn and I wanted to learn the gender of our baby naturally, when it was born.

Ultrasound pictures

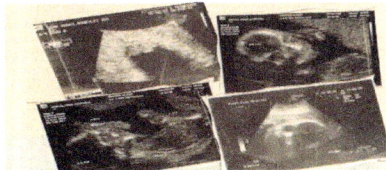

Whilst my body was transforming elegantly into motherhood, I needed to attend to the related practicalities and began to wear pregnancy clothes that I bought in the Philippines. I topped these up with clothes bought in the UK, such as maternal bras, pants, trousers, jeans, and a coat. We also bought items that would be necessary once our baby was born: cribs, a Moses basket, unisex clothes for babies of three to six months, socks, shoes, hats, blankets, a growbag, bibs, pacifiers, milk bottles, sterilisers, a milk warmer, a baby bath, soap, body wash, lotion, talcum powder, a baby towel, a pushchair and car seat, nappies, nappy socks, baby wipes, and baby bags. It was a great fun preparing for a dream that was about to come true when I finally became a mother.

First-born child

Alwyn bought a two-bedroom maisonette in North-West London in 2002, which was to become our first family home as we settled into our new environment. My journey to the Royal Free was by underground and took an hour. I kept my appointments with the midwife at the Royal Free too, as it did not make sense to move hospitals in the middle of my pregnancy period. I decided to start maternity leave two weeks before the expected birth, in order to relax and enjoy the time before I became a mother. This was the advice of the midwife, which I later realised made a lot of sense.

My due date was towards the end of September, but I had already prepared my baby bag and suitcase just in case of an unexpected early delivery, as advised. My belly towards the end of the trimester was huge and heavy, which made it hard to sleep at night. I could not lie on my back anymore as my breathing was restricted by the baby pressing on my diaphragm. In addition, the baby was constantly kicking my belly which was exciting, but which woke me up. In preparation for the birth, I bought classical music to play, which was apparently good for the baby. I also spent time talking to my baby as I was told that communication is effective in strengthening the bond between the parents and the child.

As a student nurse, I was exposed to the maternity unit where I saw mothers giving birth and I cared for them from post-partum delivery to discharge. Therefore, I did have some knowledge of what to expect. However, no one can really know until one has experienced it for oneself: one of the lessons of life I want to share with my readers. Knowledge is a completely different matter from personal experience.

Anyway, I knew there were false contractions and true contractions, but I was still unsure of the difference when I experienced them myself. In addition, I had seen how painful it could be to deliver the baby but did not know the magnitude of the pain until I experienced it. I thought my contractions were true ones, but they were not. I constantly monitored myself but the baby did not arrive on the due date, nor on a few days after that. I was therefore booked into the hospital so that the birth could be induced.

I prayed that I would give birth before induction day as I wanted as natural a birth as possible. My prayer was answered as I began what is known as a continuous contraction, meaning that I should give birth a few days before my scheduled induction. This prompted Alwyn to take me to the hospital immediately. The journey was at least forty-five minutes, so the timing was essential. I could not think of anything worse than giving birth in a car. However, God took care of me and we arrived safely at the hospital. I was examined on arrival and was told to stay at the hospital as I could give birth at any time.

I was in continuous pain and I chose gas to alleviate this, which I had to inhale several times. The gas made me fall asleep and my contractions stopped. When I woke up the next day, to my surprise I discovered I had inhaled a whole tank of gas. Given that my contractions had stopped I was advised to have an uphill walk on nearby Hampstead Heath or to eat spicy foods like curry as natural inducements, which I did.

That night, my contractions started again, this time more painful than ever. I was apparently allowed an epidural but this could not be administered so close to birth as it may have paralyzed my hip area affecting the force of my contraction. In any case, my labour was intensely slow and my baby was showing signs of distress. The team looking after me therefore decided to induce and to break my waters to facilitate the start of the normal birthing process.

I was really exhausted and tired and, given that my baby was in distress, Alwyn and I made the decision that I should have an emergency caesarean instead as advised by the maternity team. As soon as consent was given, I was wheeled to the operating table. Alwyn was allowed to stay in the operating room, praying, holding my hand, and talking to me while I was having the operation. It was such a comforting and reassuring experience having him next to me, giving love and support in my time of need.

At 15:35 on 5 October 2002, I finally gave birth. It was such a relief and comfort to hear the baby cry as soon as it was out of my womb. The pain that I endured was almost cancelled out by the sound and sight of our baby. The suffering was worth it in the end, when we were reassured that our baby girl was healthy and strong with no complications. She had light brown skin, weighed 7.3 lbs, with a caput head due to the long labour, some hair and nails, and looked like an angel.

New-born baby

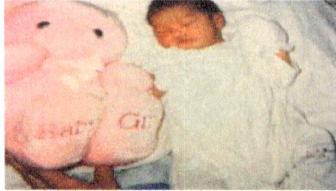

It was a joy to have such a wonderful baby in answer to my prayers to God. I was thankful for all my family and friends who were praying for me, Alwyn, and the baby, and grateful for all my friends patiently waiting in the hospital to see me and the baby. When I was back on the ward for my post-partum recovery, I was thrilled to see Imelda Chi and Armie.

Visitors on my first day post-partum

My baby and I were given our own room by the maternity matron, for which I was grateful. Ever since the birth, my baby had been with me. This is in contrast to the Philippines where babies are placed in a nursery away from their mothers. After being transferred back to the ward I had an endless stream of visits from friends and colleagues. Coincidentally, Alwyn had been scheduled his long-awaited hernia operation for my first day back on the ward, which was a great success and much relief. It was hilarious seeing us both in our hospital gowns at the same time.

I breastfed our baby girl each time she cried, which was every two to four hours. It was a great benefit to have her by my side, which strengthened the bond with her. However, I could also see the advantages of the nursery system in the Philippines, which allowed the mother to have some rest after the birth, especially after having a painful caesarean, which made it difficult to move for some days after.

Although I assumed that my baby was taking in sufficient milk, I was mistaken. She later became jaundiced which turned out to be the result of dehydration. Alwyn and I were both devastated to discover this. I was upset for having made a mistake that had led to my baby's poor health.

She was given phototherapy treatment immediately, whereby all her body except for eyes and genitals was subjected to coloured light. This was repeated several times a day for a few days until the jaundice disappeared. In addition, she was given bottle milk as an alternative to breast feeding to ensure she drank enough liquid. I was taught how to use a breast pump so that I could store and use the milk instead of milk formula.

However, I had some trouble using the pump, so had to continue using formula.

This was not a good start for my experience of motherhood but I always look on the bright side of life. In the end, our baby recovered and we were discharged from hospital. I was reassured that all would be fine, and that there would be a health visitor to check the progress of my baby and me at home, and was grateful that our baby's development would be monitored.

We decided to call our daughter Claire Margaret. My mother's name is Clarita and Claire is the English equivalent. Alwyn's mother was called Margaret. Claire became the centre of our lives, bringing us lots of joy, and we looked forward to an extraordinary life.

I was extremely anxious about breast feeding Claire and was advised to continue with the bottle milk alternative. Although I took care to follow the instructions, I was constantly watching Claire's physical appearance. Frequent nappy changes were a good sign that she was adequately nourished, and her weight was increasing, as measured by the health visitor. I was pleased that I was doing the right thing for Claire and glad that I did not give up breast feeding entirely as I enjoyed that experience, mainly for reasons I mention below.

Sleepless nights and the unpredictable behaviour of my baby were life-changing experiences. You can never plan when or why your baby will cry or, worst of all, when she will become unwell. As soon as Claire cried, I had to find out and eliminate the cause of her unhappiness. I gave her milk in case she was hungry; I changed her nappy in case she was wet and had done a poo. If she was cold I gave her a hug and warm blanket to make her comfortable. In contrast, she may have been too warm, in which case I removed the grow bag or blanket. However, she may have been crying because she was ill, so I took her temperature — or she may have been teething. All these actions can make a huge difference to a happy and growing child.

However, it was 24-hour care. It only stopped when the baby slept; it was therefore a good idea for me to sleep at the same time as the baby in order to rest. Otherwise, I would have become exhausted with non-stop work and mentally and physically ill. I obviously wanted to prevent this, as I would no longer be able to care for my baby. I was advised to look after myself by resting when not looking after the baby and to stay connected to my friends and family.

I had no family in the UK and Alwyn's family lived far away too. We had recently moved to North-West London so we were also away from work colleagues. I had had no chance to make new friends near our home as I was too busy working before Claire was born. I wish I could have turned back the clock and made friends near our home as they would then have been able to support me in those early difficult days of being a new mother.

However, I thanked God that I survived those early days of motherhood, and that I did not suffer from post-natal depression as many new mothers do. Despite being on my own, I did manage to keep in touch by telephone with my UK friends as well as with my family in the Philippines. Alwyn was also a great help as he was on paternity leave for two weeks. Even when he returned to work he was able to help with the baby, giving me some respite.

In contrast with my situation, new mothers in the Philippines always have the support of their family and friends. In Filipino culture, people who you can trust are always available to give you a helping hand, and this can reduce the pressure of being a mother for the first time. This gives you time to rest and recover while your family helps out with cooking, cleaning, and other household chores.

As the days passed, it was wonderful to see Claire grow and develop. After two weeks she smiled for the first time and was able to lift her head after three weeks. When she was two months old, she laughed, reached for things, and made babbling sounds. She first slept through the night after three months. After four months, she could pull herself up and had her first experience of teething. This can be painful, with swollen gums, a high temperature, and drooling of saliva. The discomfort can be lessened by pain killers and teething toys to bite on.

Claire was able to sit and roll over after five months and started soft feeding at six. She was able to hold her first spoon and drank from a beaker after seven and eight months, respectively. At ten months, she was able to feed herself and crawl on her knees. She finally took her first step aged thirteen months. I was lucky to have witnessed these special milestones in her development.

Crawling baby Claire

The most memorable event in Claire's life to date was the celebration of her first birthday. Alwyn and I invited all our family, neighbours, and friends to join us on this special day. It was a feast to remember, with birthday cake, noodles, hotdogs, a pork and chicken BBQ, drinks, and a lot more. Claire blew out the candles on her birthday cake while everyone was singing her first birthday song. It was a fantastic day for us all.

Giving birth and looking after my child with my husband was a life-changing experience for me. It was not as easy as I thought, and required stamina, resilience, and perseverance. However, the delight in seeing your child develop on a daily basis and observing the milestones of their first smile, word, crawl, or tooth created a deep pool of memories. Each milestone was unforgettable and we had been part of them all, every step of the way.

Renal course

My parents visited us in the UK for the first time and helped to look after Claire. It was a dream come true for my mother, her first time abroad. You cannot imagine the joy my parents felt on seeing their granddaughter for the first time. The sight of Claire reminded them of when I was a baby myself. Once they were settled here, I showed them the many attractions of London, which they really enjoyed. They were with us for six months before flying back to the Philippines.

Before my maternity leave, I had applied to study for the renal course, so I was mentally prepared to begin this once I went back to work. This was incredibly difficult as I was also writing this book at the time, as well as looking after Claire. But I was helped in having my parents here for support. At the time I was young, ambitious, and full of beans and I knew I could take on all this work.

The renal post-graduate course was essential for someone like me who wanted to specialise in renal nursing. The course would give me deeper knowledge of renal anatomy, physiology, diagnosis, treatment options etc, and was vitally important if I wanted to progress as a specialist. I began this at the Royal Free after my few months of maternity leave.

However, I was shocked to discover that my place on the course had been given to three new Irish nurses. My appeal to the development nurse who had allocated these positions was turned down. However, following a further appeal to more senior management, my place on the course was reinstated, which I regarded as just and fair. With the help of my parents, I was able to combine full-time work with studying for my course.

I graduated in 1997 in the Philippines after four years of study for a B.Sc. in Nursing and was thrilled to be studying once again. The course was at King's College London, one day a week for a few months. It was my first time at a UK university so I was excited to be embarking on this new learning experience. When the course started, I met a couple of friends from the Royal Free who were also working on renal cases.

One of them was Marsha who has remained a friend as I write this book.

The teaching style was different to that in the Philippines. Here, we were taught in classrooms and given a research assignment to be submitted at the end of the course. The research was based on our clinical experience: what interventions did I make at the time, and why? How could I improve on this in my future work and what recommendations would I make? The arguments had to be based on evidence from research using the excellent reference literature available to us.

As renal nurses, we were also allocated to work in the various areas of expertise — haemodialysis, peritoneal dialysis, and pre- and post-transplant care — to experience different treatments and patient care. We were given mentors to guide us through these various competencies. The completion of this practical work was required in addition to the research assignment.

Completing the course was a tremendous achievement and I enjoyed experiencing a new way of learning. In addition I was able to apply this knowledge during the practical work undertaken as part of the course, providing excellent care for my patients. I thoroughly enjoyed the whole experience and it prepared me for any future courses.

Acute dialysis unit

My last placement on the course was at the acute haemodialysis unit at the Royal Free Hospital, where I learned to treat patients through haemodialysis. I continued to work in this unit once the course ended and never went back to the renal transplant ward. Here, I worked with two ward managers, a few F-grade senior nurses, band E and D nurses, a healthcare assistant, cleaners, and a dialysis technician.

There were four shifts — early, late, long day, and twilight — which were allocated on a rota basis, normally two or three months in advance. Each shift required a combination of various skills while looking after the renal patients. The service ran from Monday to Saturday, with an on-call staff rota for Sundays for cases of patients requiring emergency haemodialysis.

The acute haemodialysis unit was for recently diagnosed patients requiring either permanent or temporary dialysis and for those with end-stage renal damage requiring permanent treatment. These latter patients generally needed treatment between two and four times a week, depending on the individual cases.

Every shift began with a handover where you were brought up-to-date with each patient. For example, we were told which patients needed additional care such as a blood transfusion and antibiotics; or more intensive monitoring for patients who were very ill. This handover was generally given by the nurse in charge, and everyone on duty then knew what to expect on the shift. After handover, we were assigned to work in a group of both senior and junior nurses in order to give a good balance of the skills needed.

There was a great community spirit among the staff, who came from various cultural backgrounds. We often brought in our own countries' foods to share with the rest of the team, we gathered together for birthdays, and everyone attended the Christmas party, which was great fun.

After my parents had returned to the Philippines, I requested a more flexible working week in order that I could spend more time with my daughter. It took much deliberation from HR to grant me this, and it seemed that such a request was uncommon, which I found hard to understand. However, I was grateful to be allocated a permanent twilight shift, which meant I could look after Claire during the day and Alwyn in the evening until bedtime.

Royal Free Acute Haemodialysis Team

The whole team, including the nurses in charge, was fun, friendly, and helpful. It was diverse, with members from different backgrounds and religions. There was always someone on hand to mentor or supervise you, so I never felt alone. Despite the extremely busy environment, team members were always ready to greet you with a smile and kind words.

Colleague and a friend

The flexible twilight shifts allowed me take care of Claire too. On Mondays, Wednesdays, and Fridays I worked from 5pm until 12.30am. I took Claire to work with me in a pushchair, together with her blanket, milk, nappies, and clothes, and had to leave home at about 3.30pm to be at work in time for my shift. I walked from home to Finchley Road tube station and walked again from the station to the Royal Free instead of catching a bus. The walk gave me exercise and Claire enjoyed looking at the scenery.

There were often delays on the tube, so I had to make sure I gave myself plenty of time to get to work. I also had to prepare myself for any changes in the weather and had a rain cover for the pushchair. Claire's mood could be unpredictable on the tube journey and, as a parent, you just have to accept this as part of the experience of having a young baby. If Claire cried on the tube, I gave her milk.

Sometimes, Claire's crying would annoy other passengers who could be rude to us. Once, when I found it difficult to make her stop, I read her a story. Some of the passengers gave me a nasty look and told me to control my baby's crying. I thought this was really inconsiderate! In contrast, however, some people were kind and helped me with the pushchair on the stairs of the tube stations.

Before my shift started at 5pm, Alwyn would meet me at the Royal Free and looked after Claire. After a goodbye kiss I would run off to start work. It was a difficult task to work and bring up a child at the same time. There were other options, such as employing a childminder or using a nursery, but Alwyn and I preferred to look after Claire ourselves, in order to be part of her growth and development. It was difficult bringing up a child and working at the same time. The sacrifice was not easy but was worth it in the end.

On some occasions, Alwyn could not meet me as he had a meeting at his office, so I had to arrange alternative childcare. When this happened, my friend Marsha at work would look after Claire until Alwyn arrived. It was such a great help to have a kind and trustworthy friend on hand. Marsha's husband was also very understanding and it was convenient that they lived close to the hospital.

My friend Marsha and I

Marsha was a special person and I was lucky to have such a wonderful friend who would give a helping hand without even being asked, come rain or shine.

Asthma

Unfortunately, Claire suffered from asthma, eczema, and sebaceous hair, conditions that were difficult to manage at such a young age. We realised she suffered from asthma after she had difficulty breathing, leading to a couple of hospital admissions. A chest x-ray confirmed the diagnosis. Some of her attacks were horrendous and one day she coughed continuously, which was not relieved by the maximum recommended use of a salbutamol inhaler every four hours. She quickly became unwell, pale, and lethargic; her breathing was shallow and wheezing. It was horrible to see my daughter suffer at such a young age. As a nurse, I was trained to stay calm and not to empathise with my patients; but as a mother confronting an emergency situation, what could I do? I had to take immediate medical action before it was too late.

Praying helped, and I took Claire to our local GP straight away, where she was given steroids and further inhalers. However, her condition did not improve and seemed to get worse, so the GP arranged for an ambulance to take us to the nearby hospital. Claire was immediately placed in the resuscitation room for monitoring and potential intubation. Here, she received oxygen, more steroids and more inhalers until her condition stabilised. She was moved to the children's ward for monitoring and was only discharged after a further few days.

As a mother, it was frightening and heartbreaking to see my child gasping for breath and fighting for her life. As a paediatric nurse in the past, I had seen many ill children but it was a different matter when it was my own child experiencing unbearable pain. No one really knows what it is like to suffer unless you have experienced it yourself.

Having a kind heart is essential for all healthcare workers. It is important to remember to deal with patients compassionately, whatever the cost. This can easily be forgotten for routine care, but you should always remind yourself of the purpose of your vocation.

Chapter 4

Watford Renal Unit

Chronic haemodialysis

Claire continued having mild to severe asthma attacks, which prompted me to look for work in a hospital closer to where we lived. This would be in the best interests of our family and the health of our daughter and would make it easier for me to be with Claire in case of an emergency. Alwyn's job was based in town and he could not easily change jobs. He was supportive and fully understood my decision to look for an opportunity nearby.

I soon found two vacant positions for a haemodialysis nurse, one at Northwick Park and one at the Watford Renal Unit. After making informal visits to both sites, I decided to apply for the post in Watford, which gave a better first impression, although the money was not as good as at the Royal Free as I would lose my London allowance. With the help of God, I had a successful interview and started work in Watford in January 2003.

I started as a Band D nurse but then moved to Band E which had been agreed at the interview, since I had all the necessary skills and qualifications for the role. Following my renal course, I was meant to have applied for a Band E position in the Royal Free renal transplant ward, but I didn't as I was not keen on the working environment on that particular ward.

The chronic haemodialysis ward in the Watford renal unit had long day shifts, which meant working from 7am to 8pm three days a week. There was also an additional day shift once every four weeks, taking the total to the contracted thirty-seven hours. There were 21–22 dialysis beds which meant that 42–44 patients received dialysis on each shift. The service ran Monday to Saturday with at least seven staff having a mixture of skills: one charge nurse and at least three nurses plus healthcare assistants. Both staff and patients were from very diverse backgrounds.

Next to the haemodialysis unit was the Busy Bees' Nursery, which was a great selling point for us as it meant we had a convenient childcare solution. I was grateful to have been given a childcare-friendly working week of Thursday to Saturday, which meant that Claire was left in the hands of the nursery staff for two days a week. Although I would have preferred to look after her myself, I did not have any choice at the time.

My heart was broken every time I left Claire in the nursery as she could never settle and was always crying. She was ill most of the time with a fever and a bad cough. Since the nursery would not admit children who were ill, I had to take time off work to look after Claire at home instead. The situation improved when my parents returned to the UK as they were able to look after her at home rather than her going to the nursery.

The nursery was costly and since Claire could not settle there, it was much better that her grandparents could look after her. They could provide more genuine love than the nursery staff and would form bonds with her that would last forever. Claire also had more freedom to move about at home, where it was more relaxed, and had the best homemade foods on offer.

Patients and staff experience

Chronic haemodialysis is a term used for renal patients in a stable condition with end-stage renal failure. Watford was one of the satellite renal units providing this service for patients aged eighteen to over ninety. The patients came from a very wide range of racial and ethnic backgrounds: white British, Filipino, Indian, Pakistani, and black African, as well as from a range of economic classes. Some were mentally ill or suffered from dementia or Alzheimer's. Some were fit enough to be able to work and earn a living; others were retired or unfit for work. Several of the patients had led a comfortable existence and were therefore shocked to receive a diagnosis which would greatly change their life.

It was hard being a patient on dialysis, regardless of who they were, as they had to receive treatment for four hours on three days a week. Treatment was often unproblematic but there could be complications such as hypotension, cramps, and infections. In addition they had to adhere to a special renal diet and watch their fluid intake to help avoid these complications. Haemodialysis treatment was used to prolong life. But it could create longer-term complications such as heart failure, bone disease, vascular problems, etc, which could lead to death. Patients were susceptible to potentially fatal infections if not treated immediately.

There was a great sense of community in the Watford renal unit between the staff and patients. There was also a chance to meet the family and friends of the patients who visited them during treatment. These were often great company as they tried to raise the spirits of the patients. One of the disadvantages, however, was that this sense of community could lead the nurses to become too attached to the patients. We got to know some patients very well after treating them for years, only to see them deteriorate and eventually die. This had an adverse effect on the general mood within the ward, on patients and staff alike. This mood could last for days and it was not easy to raise spirits.

Some patients, who were relatively fit, were encouraged to have a transplant and to be put on the waiting list for either a dead or live donor. Others, however, were not deemed suitable for a transplant and would therefore be on dialysis for the rest of their lives. In my opinion, a transplant was preferable for younger and fitter patients as it would lead to a much better quality of life.

It was extremely sad to see patients waiting desperately for a transplant, from either a live or dead donor. For various reasons they often had to wait a long time. I worked in the Watford renal unit for seven years and I can count the number of patients who remained on dialysis the whole time on my fingers. The rest either received a transplant or died during the time they were receiving dialysis.

The lesson is that life is unpredictable and can change for the worse at any time, irrespective of class and status. However, we are able to show love, kindness, and respect for each other, which makes living worthwhile. These actions are free and make a positive impact on the society we live in.

Haemodialysis picture with colleagues

Colleagues and friend

The staff I worked with at Watford were amazing: really friendly, supportive, and considerate, including the manager. It certainly was not perfect, but the sense of being part of a team made it a special place to work. There were times that we were understaffed, but we managed to look after our patients by helping each other. This situation, however, could not continue in the long run; the ward could only run efficiently when fully staffed and it was important not to abuse the kindness of others by always having to ask them for help.

The staff deserved better and should not have suffered from the constant struggle to be fully staffed. Unfortunately, the situation got worse rather than better. It led to low morale among the staff and a neglect of some of the essential tasks at the end of the shift due to exhaustion. Some seemed to be on the brink of collapse after years of overwork but they had to continue working in order to support their families. There was no excuse for not trying to improve our working conditions.

The understaffing was not unique to the renal unit at Watford. On other wards, staff were leaving and replaced by agency nurses. Some overseas staff had no choice but to continue due to the provisions of their work permits. Although a UK salary was higher than that in their own countries, this did not mean that they had to accept poor working conditions. I feared that if a new overseas nurse complained about overwork, she would lose her job. Staff shortages were a continuous problem. Sickness cover was provided by other members of the team working overtime, although this did mean more money.

It was not always the case that shortages were covered by a regular staff member. A vicious circle developed. Nurses doing the extra work required became exhausted and took sick leave, leading to further shortages. I heard that some staff left because the pay of a regular nurse was less than for agency nurses. And agency nurses did not have the ongoing responsibility of full-time nurses and were therefore under less pressure.

It is not good enough to say that financial security is the only thing that matters; health workers must also have enthusiasm and motivation to follow their vocation. If this is not the case, how can it be addressed? Have managers been listening to those with concerns? Will any action be taken?

One of the other reasons staff were leaving Watford was the lack of a London allowance, in contrast to the nearby Northwick Park. Many nurses looking for work would therefore choose Northwick Park rather than Watford. One of Watford's selling points was that the unit was willing to take on applicants with no haemodialysis experience. But training a new nurse takes times and increases the pressure on the senior nurses already working there. Even then, newly qualified staff would often leave after training for better opportunities elsewhere.

Despite these working conditions, the staff always found ways to entertain themselves. All staff were invited to attend the Christmas festivities, a chance to get together and celebrate achievements and successes. However, these celebrations could not disguise the underlying working conditions that still needed to be addressed. I hope that one day nurses find the courage to speak out to management without repercussions. If they do, maybe a solution will be found to improve both the working conditions and patient care.

Chapter 5

Post-natal depression

In 2006 my younger sister came to live with us while she was studying for her master's degree in computing at London Metropolitan University. It was a delight to have her stay and for her to be able to spend time with us. She had studied hard in the Philippines and received an award on graduation. She later found a job, married her boyfriend, and then moved to the UK as a highly qualified migrant worker.

She found an excellent well-paid job as a TV programmer at Sony in Hampshire. She was able to recommend that her husband work there and he found a job there too. Very soon, we heard that they were expecting their first child, which did not surprise us, and we wished them success and gave them our blessings.

One day she told us that she must move to Hampshire to be nearer her place of work, which made perfect sense. It was an exciting time for her and her husband: the anticipation of being a first-time mother and moving into their new home. She continued to work during her pregnancy, while making all the necessary preparations. Her baby was due in the autumn and our parents were making the effort to come over at that time.

Her baby girl was born via an emergency caesarean after a long labour which was causing the baby distress. It was such a relief to hear that her daughter was delivered safely and that my sister was recovering well. We returned to our London home while my parents stayed at my sister's. After a few days in hospital, my sister was discharged.

While at home I received a call from my mother and brother-in-law saying that my sister was suffering from mastitis, an inflammation of the breast due to infection. It was extremely painful and she was advised to take painkillers. However, she was later admitted to hospital for further treatment. Worse was to come as she contracted an MRSA infection while in hospital. I could not believe what was happening to her nor understand what she must have been going through, being in an isolation ward and away from her new-born baby.

Her pain was so intense that she was given morphine and codeine, very strong painkillers. Later, I discovered that she was suffering from post-partum depression, feeling apathetic and crying non-stop. I had obviously heard of this but had never met anyone who was suffering from it.

I was heartbroken to hear this incredibly sad news about my sister. As the days passed, her condition worsened, and she was taken to the baby and mother unit at the hospital for closer monitoring. When I visited her there, I realised how ill she was and sympathised with her situation. I could not imagine why she was suffering given all the support from her husband, sister, and parents around her.

It was only then that I learned that post-partum depression is common in the UK. Why were there so many similar cases in the mother and baby unit? What can be done to avoid this? And how can we reduce the stigma of poor mental health more generally? In the unit were mothers who rejected or could not look after their babies, and mothers who were suicidal or delusional. Despite her condition, my sister was at least able to look after her daughter.

The experience of seeing my sister in that condition shocked my whole family and was a difficult situation to manage. Compared to physical illness, mental illness is hard to treat. I had never felt so paralyzed in my life, being unable to help. I could do nothing but leave her in the hands of the professionals and pray for her recovery.

Chapter 6

Mother, wife, friend, and teacher

Birth of a second child

It did not take long before I was expecting another baby, which was great news for us. Our original plan was to have at least four children as we wanted a big, happy family, although accepting, too, that whatever happened would be God's will. At the time we were just glad that God had blessed us with another child, in contrast to some women desperate for children but unable to conceive. We were therefore thankful to God for this wonderful gift.

I wanted a two-year gap between my first and second children as they could then play together and become closer. It also meant that the second child could use all the baby stuff bought for the first child. I would not have to store it for long, therefore, before using it again. Moreover, I could look after two small children at the same time but would be able to continue my career once they had both grown and become more independent. Obviously, different families have different circumstances and opinions but our plan was working out according to God's grace and mercy.

The second pregnancy was not as difficult as the first one, which could be put down to experience and being better prepared mentally for what to expect. The huge difference, however, was having to look after Claire, now a toddler, while pregnant. She was a demanding child who loved being caressed and pampered the whole time and requiring constant attention. Moreover, she would not sleep on her own, so either Alwyn or I had to go to bed with her until she fell asleep, and only after that could we rest after an exhausting day.

Having a toddler while pregnant, working full-time, and managing the home required great multitasking skills. Alwyn and I had to work as a team, but it was not easy for me who was generally in charge of running the home. But life must carry on, whatever the weather, and we came through.

This was what made life in England different to that in the Philippines, where I would probably have had a nanny, maid, and chauffeur. But, as for most middle-class earners in the UK, such luxuries were not available for us. We did not have the same privileges as richer people who were deemed more powerful, in the earthly sense, at least.

In the Philippines there was always a large network of family and friends around to help in raising your family. Therefore, in times of emergency, you could always rely on someone to look after your child for a few hours. In the UK, we lived far away from our families and I therefore had little choice but to take my daughter with me everywhere I went. It was worst when the weather was bad or I had a doctor's appointment.

I could not complain, however, as this was the life in the UK that I had signed up for, and I just had to carry on like everyone else. But I could not help thinking what it would have been like to raise a family in another country. Was there anything that could be done to make things better in the UK? The one great advantage I had over many others was that my parents visited us in the UK and helped us out. This was a real bonus: it did not happen all the time but was better than nothing at all. We were also occasionally helped by my father-in-law and his wife who came over from Northern Ireland to visit us.

I was overdue for my second pregnancy, as I was for my first. Again, I was given an induction date and regular appointments for routine tests. I would have preferred a normal delivery but the maternity team suggested a caesarean instead — normal for someone like me who had already had a caesarean.

I was given a routine test by my gynaecologist and help to induce the start of the birthing process. This was successful and, soon after, my contractions began and my waters broke while I was still in hospital. My contractions became more painful but the gas I was given did not help at all. The pain was more intense than in my first pregnancy. Despite my contractions, my uterus was not opening quickly enough, causing the baby distress. The maternity team acted swiftly and I was advised to have an emergency caesarean to prevent any harm to my baby.

I signed the consent form and was taken to the operating table immediately. Alwyn was with me, which was a real blessing. I was put to sleep for the operation, but when it was over I could not breath properly. I had never been as scared in my life. The staff noted my distress and gave me oxygen support straight away, which helped me breath but I still felt shivery and cold.

Despite these problems, I was glad the birth was over and the paediatrician told me I had given birth to a very healthy baby boy, a big relief after his distress in the womb. He had been given a dose of antibiotics to prevent any possible infection from me. Our daughter Claire was being looked after by my younger sister, so we had no worries about childcare.

We were soon discharged from hospital and I began breastfeeding immediately, which seemed to be working well. I did not want to have the same problems I had feeding Claire so I was careful and put in lots of effort to make sure I was successful: breast milk is much better than formula for the baby.

Breastfeeding has many advantages. Research has shown it is the best milk for the baby. It forms a strong bond between mother and child, which was important to you. It is cheaper, as I did not have to spend money, and more convenient in not having to prepare formula, wash, and sterilise bottles. Finally, I was able to lose weight faster.

However, there are disadvantages. A new-born baby constantly demands to be fed, which can be very tiring for the mother. With formula, anyone can feed the baby, not just the mother, which allows the mother to rest. This can be avoided by using a breast pump to express the milk. Also, because breast milk is more dilute, it takes longer to feed the baby than with formula. Finally, with a bottle it is easier to feed out of doors when it may be difficult to preserve one's dignity breastfeeding.

We named our second baby John Lambert Orr, a name taken from his grandfathers: John from his paternal grandfather and Lambert from Lamberto, my father's name. Apart from having different sexes, our two children also had very different personalities, and we loved and cared for them equally for what they were.

Baby John

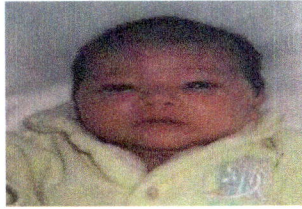

Compared to Claire who did not settle down easily, John was a quiet baby who was able to sleep in his cot alone. It was a shock when we first started changing John's nappies and were squirted with his urine! Nappy changing for Claire was more straightforward. However, it was much easier to potty train John than it was for Claire. In contrast, Claire started walking earlier than John who was happy to continue using his walker.

Motherhood is not easy but, together, we negotiated the difficulties and survived. It comes with huge responsibilities but we had prepared ourselves to face them. This would not have been possible without God's blessing and the help of our family and friends who supported us in times of need.

Work–life balance and friendship

Returning to work with two young children was not easy, as you can imagine. I loved my children and wanted to prioritise them over my career. I strongly believe that the most important thing in life is to bring up your children in a way that allows them to contribute to the good of mankind as they grow older.

For these reasons, I asked my managers if I could have a more flexible working arrangement. This would mean continuing to work at a less qualified level to maintain my nursing licence rather than having to give up work entirely. It was important to maintain some experience as practices can sometimes change dramatically. Working on a part-time basis was therefore better than not working at all.

My managers allowed me to work fifteen hours a week part-time: a long day shift on Saturdays and a shorter day shift on Wednesdays. I worked part-time for a long period while bringing up my two children and was grateful for the flexibility. I looked after the children while Alwyn was at work whereas Alwyn did so on Saturdays, when I worked.

However, working part-time meant that my career progression was put on hold. Being a mother was a full-time job in itself and I accepted that I could not continue moving ahead in my career as well as being a mother. But being a wife and mother were the most precious things I have ever done, the most rewarding jobs in the world. Being part of my children's lives as they grew up was something I was very proud of as a parent.

Motherhood was challenging and required good communication, the management of expectations, conflict resolution, and the building of trust to overcome some of the difficulties I encountered daily. However, it was a great training ground and the skills I learned were extraordinary.

As the children grew up, they needed to be in a more social environment to keep them active. We first attended the baby and toddler groups attached to local churches where I met other local mothers and their children. These groups were run by volunteers who were mothers themselves and who wanted to make a positive impact on the community. The activities catered for new-born babies as well as young children. Being part of the local community was an excellent experience.

Our children were enrolled at a pre-school nursery at age three. This was only for three hours a day but was still better than nothing. They were able to make new friends which would stimulate their growth and development. It also allowed me some respite and time to look after myself. Although the school was not totally free, three hours of education were funded by the government to support young families.

I was raised as a Catholic whereas Alwyn was a Methodist. These religious differences never harmed our relationship despite the strictness of some Catholic practices. We learned how to compromise and talk through any problems before they escalated into something more serious. Open and honest communication has helped our relationship to flourish and made us into a great team in everything we do.

From the beginning, we had to decide which of the churches best suited our needs. However, as soon as we had children we settled on a local one, which was most convenient and practical. We soon became part of the church community and found our fellow members of the congregation friendly and helpful. Children were able to attend a service on Sunday morning where they were taught the gospel in a way best suited to their age group. Living in Christian faith in Christ became part of our family life.

I mention these experiences as I considered them part of God's plan for our family. In order for our children to be enrolled in one of the best primary schools in the area, we needed a letter of recommendation from our minister and a record of good attendance at the local Church of England church. This was also required when we enrolled them in secondary school. Looking back, our children would not have been able to go to the CoE school if we had not attended St Edmund's Church. This is proof that miracles can happen. Even though God's plan is not clear immediately, it is so eventually.

Our children began their primary school life aged four at the Holy Trinity Primary School in Northwood. Here, they were able to develop additional skills, to socialise, and build their confidence by taking part in ballet, swimming, football, and drama classes. It was also an opportunity for me to join a community of local mothers who were all doing their best for their children and local area.

Some of my best memories of the school run were the chats I had with other mums after our hectic mornings preparing our children for school. We were on common ground, sharing the same experiences, irrespective of our various backgrounds and we chatted together without judgement. We sometimes arranged coffee mornings or activities such as jogging.

I became friends with some of the mothers, including Lucy and Karen, who were great help with childcare or other matters. I also participated in voluntary work such as fundraising or assisting on school trips, for example. Outside school, in the wider local community, we helped in the scouts or other church activities.

In addition to the friends I met through school, I had others I met in the wider community, who are still friends at the time of writing this book. These, too, helped with childcare, gave general advice, or were just around when I didn't want to be alone. I can't mention everyone here but I have listed them all in the acknowledgements as an appreciation of my thanks.

The school runs became a routine in my daily life and I loved seeing the joy on my children's faces as I collected them from school, although they could be annoyed if I were late. Being there for them made them feel secure and loved and I considered myself fortunate as some parents, for a variety of reasons, were not able to spend so much time with their children at this age.

Alwyn or I always found time to attend school events such as sports days, nativities, concerts, dances, or plays. Sometimes, due to pressure of work, only one of us could attend but being able to support our children in this way made a huge difference. Our children appreciated the effort we made as shown by the joy on their faces during the performances.

Birthday parties were the most highly anticipated events and it was essential that our children were able to go to the parties of their friends. The celebrations took the form of a wide range of themes such as Cinderella, pirates, clowns, film shows, baking, or sports days. They were held either in parents' houses or hired venues and it was great to be part of our children's social life.

Primary school mothers

As a mother it was really useful to pass my driving test and have my own car since part of my role as mother was acting as a taxi driver for my children! They had to be taken to various activities every day except Sundays. They were very fortunate to be able to do so as I did not have these opportunities when I was a child. I wondered if this impacted on my development. Would I have developed other talents if I had had such opportunities at a young age?

The variety of extracurricular activities seemed endless. Sports included swimming, football, cricket, tennis, netball, hockey, horse riding, cycling, climbing, martial arts, kayaking or other water sports. They were able to learn to play the recorder, flute, violin, piano, and trumpet; or learn ballet, tap dancing, street dancing, singing, drama, or art. They had an opportunitiy to take part in many different activities and I was grateful to God that we were able to afford it.

As with Claire, John also suffered from asthma, eczema, and sebaceous hair. On one exceptionally difficult day, we had to take him to A&E where he was taken immediately to the resuscitation room for potential intubation. He was wheezing and struggling to breath; he was pale and tired and his pulse was rapid. As a mother it was frightening as I knew that such symptoms could be fatal if not treated quickly.

After this initial treatment he was admitted to the children's high dependency unit where he was given steroids, a magnesium drip and inhalers. Being unable to help, I felt paralyzed. Seeing John fighting for his life was heartbreaking and an extremely challenging time for the family. Thankfully, our prayers were answered and he was eventually discharged. Obviously, it is common that children become ill at times but no one can predict when and this should be taken into account when planning your life. Sleepless nights are common, especially when children are ill, but you still need the energy to carry out your roles as a parent the following day.

I will end this section by saying that finding the correct work–life balance is extremely difficult. My advice is that each of us must establish what our priorities in life are. In my nursing work, I have always strived for the highest possible standards of care; this would not have been possible working full time as well as caring for a family. Therefore, I chose to work part time. However, other mothers may have made a different choice if it was possible for them to share parental responsibilities more equally with their husband. I have no regrets making the choice I did. I had an amazing time bringing up my children; it created a long-lasting relationship with them which will last for the rest of my life and which cannot be measured financially.

First family holiday in the Philippines

Due to work and family commitments, it took a long time before we arranged a visit to the Philippines. Taking a family of four is also costly, so we had to save for some time before we could make the trip. Given that my immediate family were all in the UK and that my parents visited frequently from the Philippines, we did not need to go home as often as other Filipinos in the UK. However, in 2006 after seven years in the UK, we were given the opportunity when Claire and John were selected as bridesmaid and pageboy at my brother's wedding.

I could not attend my sister's wedding in 2004 as I was heavily pregnant and therefore unable to fly, so we did not want to miss out on another happy family event. It did, however, take great courage and determination to take two toddlers aged one and three on the long flight to the Philippines.

I was partly responsible for introducing my brother to his future wife, Armie. He had been in contact with a female friend of his in the UK. When he came over to visit us, he arranged a date with her hoping that it may lead to a more long-term relationship. Unfortunately, however, when they met there was little chemistry and they did not keep in touch after this meeting. After this disappointment, I introduced my brother to my friends Armie and Imelda to keep him busy while he was in the UK, while I was looking after my family. In addition, I thought it would do my brother good to meet some single people. This introduction led to Armie and my brother falling in love and to the wedding we were attending in the Philippines.

Anyway, returning to the preparations for our exciting trip home with two young children. Before the trip I had to make sure that we had travel insurance and that our passports were up to date. We had the necessary vaccinations and gathered together all the emergency medications we may need for asthma and eczema, as well as paracetamol, antihistamines, and mosquito spray. The baby and toddler group at our local church were able to lend me a light double travel buggy. Having both children in the same buggy made travel much less stressful as they could both be fed in it in a busy airport lounge. I also had to make sure that nappies, wipes, and toys — as well as their milk and food — were easily accessible in my hand luggage.

Double buggy

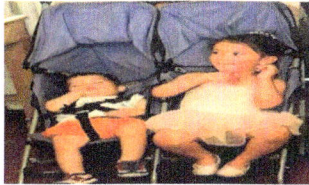

The preparations were not easy but one of my qualities is a determination to get things done rather than making excuses and putting things off. One just needs to get down to it. Preparing for a long flight and visit to the Philippines with a young family was scary, but I would rather face up to these fears rather than miss out on what was an amazing experience.

Checking in at the airport was easy as I had help from my husband. We took two items of hand luggage on board and our other items were checked in with no problems of excess weight. On board, the stewardesses were kind and gave us help heating milk and providing sickness bags. It was a great experience with excellent customer service. On the plane some of our fellow passengers looked after our children briefly, while we stretched our legs walking up and down the aisle. Although the children got bored watching children's TV, they did not make any noise and we had no complaints, even when they were constantly walking in the aisle.

Claire and John watching our plane before flying back to the UK

With God's blessing, I have always received help from people whenever I've needed it. This may be the reason for my positive outlook on life as He has never let me down. If, however, He appears to have done so, I know that He has another plan for me, which will be better than the one I desire. I have always said that things happen for a good reason, even if it doesn't feel like that at the time.

Anyway, we all survived our 24-hour flights to and from the UK. We had a wonderful time in the Philippines and thoroughly enjoyed my brother's wedding. We will cherish the memories of it for the rest of our lives.

The wedding photos of my brother and Armie

Chapter 7

Imperial Healthcare NHS Trusts

Live donation — patients experience and raising awareness

My time on haemodialysis was finally over as I embarked on a new challenging role as renal live donor transplant coordinator at Imperial Healthcare NHS Trusts. I knew that it was the right time for me to move on from the haemodialysis unit as I was getting extremely frustrated and saddened by dying patients as the months passed by. I was badly affected emotionally in this environment and I knew it was not good for my mental wellbeing. In addition, I felt that I had stopped learning and that I needed a new challenge in life. Working in haemodialysis had become a dull routine. I am a passionate nurse and if my heart was no longer in my work, I felt there was no point in continuing.

I had a successful interview for the role as renal live donor coordinator and was able to work part time in order that I could continue with my family commitments. I started this challenging role at the Hammersmith renal unit and knew that it would suit my qualities and skills. I have always been organised and efficient with a close attention to detail; a nurse with a passion to deliver the best possible patient care. There was another aspect to the role which increased my interest in it: I would finally be able to help those patients who could move on with their lives after a successful transplant. It always saddened me to lose beloved patients to kidney failure. The thought of being part of a life-changing experience was attractive to me. Professionally, I was promoted to a more senior role from Band 6 to Band 7. This involved learning specialist clinical skills which would widen my general nursing knowledge, and hence enhance my future career prospects.

This role has brought me lots of personal and professional experiences over the years. Many were very challenging which suits me as tough challenges keep me motivated. It was a privilege to be involved in such a rewarding role, saving the lives of my patients. There were lots of surprising stories involving live kidney donors. The selection process involved assessment, further investigations, and the reviews that both donor and recipient must go through in order to establish their suitability for the transplant. Many of these stories had a happy ending but there were also failures and sadness.

Patient safety was obviously the main priority, so the most important aspect of the assessment process was stringent screening. Unfortunately, some patients were unable to proceed with a transplant for medical reasons. In these cases, the emotional upset caused may have led to a referral for counselling.

The main thing I want to share with my readers is the role of God in helping me care for my patients. God has never let me down, however difficult the situation, He has always found ways to help me. When I felt overwhelmed by my workload He miraculously cleared things for me. There were miracles that I could not explain. Every patient who had a successful transplant was a blessing from God. He guided me and answered all my prayers.

There are various categories of living kidney donors. The most basic is the directed donation from a matching donor to a specific recipient. Usually, the donors are parents, children, siblings, aunties or uncles of the recipient. Husbands, wives, friends, and in-laws are classed as unrelated donors. Altruistic donors are those who donate as strangers without a specific recipient in mind. There is also paired/pooled donation available to achieve better compatibility for donor–recipient pairs.

Transplants are a complex field but information on donating is always available from your local nephrology team or from the NHSBT website.

Live donation — patients' experience and raising awareness

A story from Sharmini Byrne who donated her kidney to her beloved mum

My mother always treated her body very well throughout life, but unfortunately, she developed kidney problems around 2010. We had big plans to go to our family friend's wedding in Malaysia, but she was told that she had to start dialysis the next day, and so she told me I must go and represent her whilst she began her treatment. It was a very scary time for us – I have always had caring responsibilities towards my mother after she went blind in her 40s, so it was hard to think that something else so traumatic was happening to her.

My dad spent the next two years taking her to and from dialysis — everything changed in our household, from the food we ate on the dialysis diet to the sadness and mood of my mother who was slowly getting more and more sick. She followed the rules completely. She was in remission for cancer and, luckily, Dr Cairns was happy for her to proceed with live donation. This was the best news we could have received. I had no doubt in my mind that I wanted to be tested to be a match, and so did my father. I have a brother who suffered with kidney problems when he was a young boy, so he was unable to put himself forward.

I was very quickly contacted by the live donation team and knew I had made the right decision — in my heart and mind, there was no other way to help improve my mum's situation and, rather selfishly, improve my own situation. She was finding it difficult to walk, her temperament was tough to be around, she was grey, she was bloated. If I were a match, she would get back to being my happy mum again. I knew it would be difficult for her to get a donor on the waiting list, and I could not wait around to see her go downhill any further.

Honey spent a long time with me and dad, explaining the tests, every step of the process, and I immediately warmed to her. I felt we were in good hands. Unsurprisingly, my dad was not a suitable match, but I certainly was. I was extremely excited, but I knew my mum was upset — as I was — as she didn't want it to harm me in any way. Coming from a scientific background myself, I did not feel that I was putting myself in harm's way — the only difficult part of the decision was thinking about what would happen to my brother when he may need a kidney himself. But I had to deal with the situation now — so if mum needs it, she can have it.

I somehow managed to fly through the tests, and quite enjoyed the process. I was 31, no kids yet, climbing high in my career, so better to do it sooner rather than later. It was a beautiful August, and mum told me to go away with my friends for a little holiday, to relax and take the surgery off my mind. I had never had any surgery before, so there was a bit of anxiety, but my girls' trip soon saw that off. It also gave my nice big kidney a final send off, filled with vodka and ginger ale.

The big day soon arrived — we had about ten relatives over from Malaysia to come and help keep our spirits up for the surgery. My mum went in the night before, and my dad and uncle brought to the hospital. It was planned for 8 or 9 am and we got stuck in traffic, and the surgeon called to ask if I was on my way or having second thoughts. I cried the whole way with nerves, but still had no doubt. After arriving twenty minutes late, I was in a daze, but was very quickly hooked up and brought down to the surgeon. It was the best thing that I was late; it gave me less time to worry and just to get on with it.

When I woke up, mum was next to me on the ward. We held hands and I suddenly felt the pain of the surgery. I had never felt pain like it, I could not sit myself up, I thought my hole had opened. Now I know that this is how people feel after surgery, but I was a rookie — I pressed the morphine button, and it all went. Mum was content, calm. I had not seen her like that for a long time. It became blissful. Then another miracle happened — her best friend from dialysis got called for a kidney the same day and was on the ward next to us.

After a few nights, I wanted to go home, to have my own bed, my shower. The lovely doctor asked me to wait one more night, but I felt good enough. He sat me down and explained how I might feel now. He said mum will improve rapidly, the kidney is working, and I will see the power of what we did. He did say I may feel incredibly sad, depressed, and go downhill. The reason is that I had a healthy body and have had a major surgery with no benefit to me personally, and the recovery is harder for a donor than a recipient. He was not wrong — this happened very quickly over the next six weeks or so. I was struggling to stand up, my whole abdomen was disrupted, my core gone. I had to ask my brother or his wife to help me out of bed. It took me an hour to walk to the local shop, which usually took twenty minutes. It slowly improved, but I wish I had not underestimated how hard it is to recover after such major surgery (this was explained throughout but when you are young and invincible, you don't think about it).

Mum came home in about two weeks, and as soon as I saw her, I hugged her and bawled my eyes out. I just needed to see her get better and she looked incredible. Her lovely skin was brown again, not grey; her smile was there, she had dropped water weight. I on the other hand was a greasy slobbering mess… but I felt happy. I told her she must have a glass of wine before her new kidney suffers withdrawal symptoms — she respectfully declined as she very rarely drank.

I went back to work after eight weeks on a phased return. I felt every bump in the road, and my kind boss let me travel in at different times, by train or car so that I was not near anybody. As the surgery is around the waist area, I was hunched over, almost in protective mode to make sure nobody brushed past me. I felt fully better after around twelve weeks, upright, and doing my normal day-to-day things.

Mum went from strength to strength — we resumed a happy family life again.
She did suffer with rejection a few years later. This was a big shock to me, and I must say that I felt guilty and upset that, despite being a perfect match, it was not working properly. However, her professor assured me it wasn't my fault and rejection is entirely fixable. That picked me up — I needed to

hear it. She has had a few infections and a few overnight stays in hospital, but nothing serious. Anything was better than dialysis and near death.

Overall, it was a split-second decision that I will never regret. I hope it gives her the life she needs and deserves. I was only disappointed that I had asked the surgeon to do a bit of liposuction for me at the same time but he did not, but you can't have everything can you?

Sharmini and her mother

Live donation — patients' experience and raising awareness

One of my patient cases to share

I had a referral from one of our pre-dialysis clinics at Imperial. Apparently, the donor was the niece (aged about thirty) of the recipient, from abroad and who arrived in the UK about three months earlier. The recipient was about fifty and I had to use the interpreter service as the donor could not speak English.

The first visit involved compatibility tests and a discussion between the donor, his wife, and his niece. I noticed the large age difference between the donor and recipient and wondered why the wife had not volunteered instead of the niece. Part of the live donor discussion involves the HTA (Human Tissue Authority) requirements, where the donor and recipient are asked to provide proof of their alleged relationship. I asked them to provide passports or full driving licences as well as birth certificates that would help us trace the parents of the mother and recipient.

During the discussion, the recipient suddenly told me that the documentation I required was too difficult to obtain. For example, the donor's birth certificate was in the country she had left for the UK, and she didn't have her mother's birth certificate either. I explained that they should try to obtain these documents as the transplant couldn't go ahead without proof of the alleged relationship between donor and recipient. I also explained the laws of the HTA, which required that donations should be genuine gifts and not as the result of coercion or financial incentives.

After these initial discussions, I asked the recipient and his wife to leave the room while I asked the donor about her medical history. I assured her that the conversation would be confidential and that she could contact me by phone if she ever changed her mind about donating. An interpreter would always be available so that she would not have to rely on her relatives in London. She appeared relieved and told me she lived in her uncle's house in London. He had helped her family for many years and she wanted to repay his generosity.

Once the recipient and his wife returned to the room it was obvious that they were unhappy that I had interviewed the donor alone. The recipient wanted to know how long it would take to receive the results of the compatibility tests — these could take three to four weeks. I explained that the results would only be given to the donor but he insisted that he be given them too so he could translate them for his niece. She wanted to share the results with her uncle.

I then asked the recipient if there were any other potential live donors in case the compatibility tests were negative, such as children. His wife offered but the recipient was not keen. Although he had medically fit older children he did not want to consider them as donors. This struck me as odd given that he seemed happy to use his young niece as donor.

A few weeks later, I began to receive constant messages from the recipient asking about the results of the compatibility tests and complaining about the time taken. I explained firmly that the results would be given to his niece and that they could take up to four weeks. Once the results arrived I contacted the donor through an interpreter. As is often the case, it was difficult to contact her and I had to leave a couple of messages. Once we managed to speak she said she couldn't discuss the test results as she was in her uncle's house, so we arranged to meet in person instead. She reassured me that she was safe but I gave her my direct number in case she needed urgent help from me.

I became suspicious: firstly, about the genuine desire of the niece to donate; secondly, about the pressure exerted on her by her uncle. I voiced my concerns with my team, including the consultant, and told them I was going to meet the donor alone to establish what exactly was going on, and they were supportive.

I met the donor with an interpreter, reassuring her of my support. She explained that she wanted a private meeting as she had decided she didn't want to donate. I explained that we would do what we could to avoid putting her in jeopardy with her uncle and that any conversations would remain confidential. As a live donor coordinator, the safety and wishes of the donor were my primary duties. I was so glad to be able to prevent this young girl, and others, from donating their kidney involuntarily.

Live donation — patients' experience and raising awareness

Claire Vaizey Moore is an altruistic kidney donor

What a privilege: My journey as a kidney donor.

I had considered being a kidney donor on and off for about two years. I have given blood for many years and am on the bone marrow donor list. I carry a donor card and have always felt it was the right thing to do, so I found nothing wrong in donating organs but had thought you had to have died first.

My mother was also a regular blood donor, and I can remember going with her as a child, so it has always seemed the right thing to do.

I became aware of the idea of non-directed altruistic donation after hearing a programme on the radio and, as I looked into it, I listened to donors' stories and googled everything I could about it. It sounded like an amazing thing to do but then it went to the back of my mind. It was only when I saw a programme on television that said only a very few people are able to donate organs when they die, even if they carry a donor card (because you have to die in very specific circumstances), that I began to think about live donation again.

In June 2018 I spoke to my partner about the idea of becoming a live kidney donor. We looked at all the information we could find about kidney donation and discussed our thoughts and feelings about it. We weighed up the risks and benefits and concluded that it was the right thing for me to do. The next day, I called the transplant centre at Hammersmith hospital and spoke to Honey who was the transplant coordinator. She asked a lot of questions about my motivations for wanting to be a kidney donor. I explained that I had been lucky and that no one in my family or circle of friends had ever needed a kidney. I really felt strongly that sharing what I had with someone else was important to me.

I have had my own health issues in the past, as has my son, and we have both benefited so much from the NHS. I felt it was time to give something back if I could as I know how important good health is. I have also had several friends die of cancer and could do nothing about it. I knew that if they had needed a kidney, I would not have hesitated to give them one so why not do the same for a stranger.

Once I had spoken to Honey and she had explained the process I agreed I wanted to go ahead. The first step was to contact my GP for my medical records. Honey explained that the records would be looked at in detail and they would let me know shortly if we could move forward. If so, I would then have an appointment at the hospital for blood and kidney function tests.

I spoke to my partner and both of my sons again before filling in the forms and sending them off. I shared as much information as I could with them, and we discussed the risks to me and my reasons for wanting to donate.

The next day the hospital sent me a letter to take to my GP asking them to release my medical records. A couple of weeks later I had a call from Honey to say my GP had still not responded. After chasing them up the records were released to the renal unit and an appointment was booked for me to go for initial assessments. Honey said she would let me know as soon as the consultant gave her agreement for me to go ahead with the process.

That night Sue (my partner) and I went out for a meal and talked about what it would mean for both of us, telling the whole family and how other people might react. I was still very keen to go ahead, and Sue said she might think about it after she had seen how I got on. It felt exciting and scary at that moment.

Honey phoned a few weeks later to say the consultant was happy for me to go ahead with the assessments. It was becoming very real now. Coming home from work that night I heard a woman on the radio talking about how she had kidney failure and that a transplant had transformed her life and that she was now determined to live life to the full. This convinced me that I was doing the right thing.

It is an enormous idea to think an ordinary person like me can literally stop someone from dying by donating a kidney. It made perfect sense to me as I already volunteered for the Samaritans where we offer a listening ear and emotional support to people, and I now had a way of doing something practical as well. It will be a short interruption to my life but life changing for someone else.

There are many steps in the process towards donating a kidney, all in place to ensure that you are as safe and healthy as possible before they actually operate. Each step of the process involved a lot of waiting for appointments and tests, but this also gave me time to think things through at each step. There was never any pressure, and I always knew I could stop the process at any stage. My first appointment was for 18 September 2018. They said I would need to bring a 24-hour urine sample. That seemed a bit of a challenge but after a while you get very used to strange requests.

Now it was becoming a reality one of my sons spoke to me and expressed his concerns about how I would live with one kidney, that major surgery is really risky, and that he couldn't understand why I wanted to do such a thing. I gave him all the information I had and explained that having been ill myself I know how important it is to be healthy. We spoke about his feelings and, in the end, he said that he understood why I wanted to do it but he was still worried. We spoke again several times throughout the process. While he was never really happy about the idea, he accepted that I wanted to do this, and he would support me.

The whole process of tests and assessments took several months, including meeting with a psychologist as well as having numerous medical tests to ensure I was fit and healthy and would be able to live a healthy life with one kidney, both physically and mentally. The hospital was very good at trying to fit the appointments around my commitments. The whole day I spent in the hospital having a barrage of tests was an amazing, bewildering, and sometimes stressful experience but everyone was lovely and really made me feel that what I was doing was valuable. I have never had such a thorough medical in my life and it was really reassuring to know that I was fit and healthy and that they take such care of their donors. Honey had also explained that if they did find anything wrong during the tests, they would make sure I was referred to the right team for treatment. Seeing people in the clinic with kidney failure when I went for my appointments reinforced my conviction that I was doing the right thing.

I also attended a seminar where surgeons, consultants, past donors, and recipients spoke about the process and their experiences. It was really valuable for me as it helped me to understand not only the process but how I might feel afterwards and it gave me the chance to talk to people who had already donated. I found this helpful. It also meant I could explain to my family what would happen after the operation.

There was a lot of waiting between appointments, but each step forward made me more and more sure that I was doing the right thing. Finally, all my tests were over, and I was given the go ahead to donate a kidney. I knew about the matching runs when they look to see if there is a match with someone who needs a kidney; they also then try and trigger a chain of donations. This give me a timescale for my donation which was June 2019. It was all getting very serious now.

I had spoken to my boss and HR at work who were all very supportive so I knew that I would be paid while I recovered from surgery. The response from both work colleagues and friends varied from amazement to horror at what I was going to do. Most people admired my decision but felt they could never do it for someone they didn't know. However, several people said if it was a family member they would. I found this really confusing.

The whole process from first contacting the hospital to finally donating a kidney took nine months. On 5 June 2019 my partner and I arrived at the hospital in the early morning when I would finally donate a kidney. I was apprehensive but having had several operations knew what to expect. Reality hit when Honey arrived in the pre-admissions ward with an insulated box which would transport my kidney to the recipient. It was really strange to think that in a few hours a piece of me would be travelling in the box to another hospital and given to someone else. Even at this stage I was still assured that if I felt I couldn't go through with it that was OK. This happened at every step of the process.

They then took my weight, blood pressure, and bloods. I guessed these were OK as they then presented me with a gown, stocking and bright red socks to put on. We were told there was a slight delay as they had operated on three deceased donors that night. However, I was told not to worry and that my operation would still go ahead. Sue left just before 9 am as she had to go to work, and I went down to the theatre at 9.30. I walked down with Honey who was still holding the box.

I woke up in the recovery room to hear people talking about my blood pressure being rather low and that I needed a boost. When I opened my eyes, it was 2.30 pm. I dosed on and off. I don't remember being moved but woke properly to find myself in the high dependency unit wired to a machine with lights and bleeps everywhere. I stayed there for two days before being moved to the ordinary ward; after another day there I went home. While in the ward I met two people who had received kidneys and were recovering, and both made a point of telling me what a marvellous thing I had done and how grateful they were that people would donate even if they didn't know the recipient. This made me feel very proud. It was a good feeling, and I left the hospital feeling sore but very proud that I had donated my kidney.

I was back at work after five weeks and now, two years on, I forget that I only have one kidney and have no regrets at all. It was a positive experience for me with no lasting effects apart from a warm fuzzy feeling inside that I did the right thing.

Live donation — patients' experience and raising awareness

Raising awareness was part of my role that was crucially important in promoting organ donation. With so many people who are ill and dying while waiting for a donor, therefore, as a professional I had to do my best to spread the word about organ donation to the general public and to correct any misunderstandings about it. With the shortage of available organs, it makes sense to try and get as many donors as possible from among those who are able. The UK has an opt-out system in place whereby everyone is a registered donor on death unless they decide to opt out before. However, it is still possible for family members to refuse to allow the deceased to donate, which seems to defeat the object of the opt-out system.

There are still many people who are reluctant to donate their organs due to personal, cultural, and religious beliefs. Education is therefore an important tool in changing perspectives and for increasing the number of organs available, thereby saving lives. I was heavily involved in raising awareness across various health sectors. I gave presentations to staff and patients in my hospital about the live donation programme. I was also involved in the running of transplant seminars four times a year to raise awareness.

Promoting the programme was part of the junior nurses' education.

I was also involved in the education of external staff, such as those from the Human Tissue Authority and new independent assessors. In addition, I was in constant telephone contact with either internal or external staff requiring information. There never seemed to be enough time to deal with all the enquiries. However, my role in raising awareness of the live donation programme was important in saving many lives. The more education and awareness, the better.

Moreover, I also participated in mentoring renal course students and other healthcare professionals, such as a Sri Lankan coordinator who came to the UK to visit the transplant unit. By sharing our experiences we were able to improve the practices at other transplant centres. Again, the bottom line was a desire to raise awareness.

Picture of myself and the renal transplant coordinator from Sri Lanka

Live donation — patients' experience and raising awareness

I met a lovely family for their first appointment with me for compatibility tests and live donor discussions.

The recipient was a pre-dialysis patient in one of the referral units at Imperial. As the term suggests, pre-dialysis patients are not yet on dialysis but will soon require it as their eGFR (estimated glomerular filtration rate) is less than 20. The recipient had had kidney problems from a young age, and the time had come when his kidney functions had deteriorated to the point that he needed renal replacement therapy. The options were discussed with his nephrology consultant and he chose to explore live donation rather than dialysis.

The potential donors were his brothers in their late thirties and his mother, who all attended the meeting too. The family seemed close-knit and I had no doubt that they genuinely wished to help and make such a sacrifice for their brother and son.

Fortunately, his mother was found to be a compatible donor so the investigations were able to continue. These investigations were not altogether straightforward and further tests were necessary but, eventually, she was deemed suitable to proceed as a donor. Preparations for the operation were started. It was a happy and rewarding experience for me to be able to be part of what could be a life-changing transplant for her son.

Unfortunately, however, a small proportion of transplants fail, for a variety of reasons, and this was the case for this one. After six years of doing this kind of work, it was the first time I experienced such a failure. I was filled with sadness and had great sympathy for the family. It was a painful time for everyone involved.

The mother attended the first follow-up appointment post-donation, and she was devastated when she heard the news, so I spent most of the meeting consoling her. It was a difficult time, and it was hard to know what to say. I just listened while she cried non-stop and I offered her the hospital's counselling services for extra support. After the meeting, I spent lots of time talking to her by phone to make sure she was all right. She decided not to attend a subsequent appointment at Hammersmith as the memories it brought back were too painful, which was understandable.

After a few months, the family began to accept the situation and were able to move on. The potential recipient was referred to me for another possible live donor transplant, this time from one of his two brothers. One was discovered to be more compatible than the other and the recipient was fortunate to find a compatible donor after the failure of the first transplant.

Further tests were carried out on the potential donor and he was given the all clear to proceed. However, for personal reasons, he wished to delay the operation, a decision I completely respected. This kind of situation is challenging for me: the recipient wants the transplant as soon as possible but the donor wants to delay it until he is ready physically and emotionally. There is also the question of confidentiality. This is not a problem when the donor and recipient are honest with each other but in other cases I had to put myself in the middle and work out a plan amenable to both donor and recipient.

In this particular case, however, things worked out in the end and the donation was successful: a happy ending to such a long journey. The recipient had received the gift of life which gave him a new beginning. I was glad to have been part of this wonderful story.

Live donation — patients' experience and raising awareness

Honeylet Orr's 2019 Imperial blog to promote live donation

I am a renal live donor transplant coordinator at Hammersmith hospital and have worked for eighteen years within the NHS, including nine years in my current role at the time of writing this blog.

Currently in the UK, there are about five thousand patients listed on the deceased waiting list, and at least one patient dies every day waiting. The average waiting time is three to five years for a kidney transplant from a deceased donor.

Living kidney donors shorten the waiting time and save lives for patients with End-Stage Renal Failure (ESRF). Transplants are the best option for ESRF patients and lead to a more normal life. **We are born with two kidneys but we can survive with only one. Kidney donation operation is a safe procedure: there is a 1 in 3000 risk of death, which is similar to having an appendix removed. Live kidney donors can either be related, live related, or altruistic.**

One of the NHSBT's strategic objectives is to increase living organ donors/registrations from BAME backgrounds to meet demand. This will increase the number of transplants from these communities, which account for a third of those awaiting transplants. There is more work to be done to increase awareness within the

BAME community, and there are several current nationwide campaigns funded by NHSBT.

Some barriers against transplants are:

- Education – is it safe to proceed?
- They are against religious beliefs
- They would like their body to remain intact when they die

One of my roles as a highly autonomous nurse practitioner in the specialised area of renal live donation is promoting and raising awareness about organ donation. I am responsible for assessing potential live donors up to the point of their donation. I give expert advice and participate in education for patients and staff regarding the live donation programme. My duty of care is making sure that live donors are being supported psychologically and physically throughout the whole process, especially if they have changed their mind not to proceed for any reasons. We take the utmost care of donors over their lifetimes with regular follow-up meetings in our clinic.

What I find most challenging in my role is dealing with the complexity of the donor–recipient relationship and the family dynamics involved. It requires observation and good detective work to make sure that donors are not being coerced or being offered financial incentives to help their loved ones.

The most rewarding part of my job is seeing the recipient able to lead a normal life after the transplant, being able to eat and drink freely, and especially being free from dialysis.

I am very privileged to have such a rewarding job, surrounded by highly specialised and supportive renal consultants and surgeons who do not fail to give the best possible help to our patients.

My advice to anyone considering being a live donor is to proceed with the donor work-up tests as this will help transform the lives of many. Transplants save lives!!

Further information is available on the Organ Donation website.

Donor restructuring and house moving

In 2013 the live donor unit went through a huge restructuring in order to improve the service and reduce costs. This was a terrible time for the seven coordinators in our team as it came about unexpectedly. We were also worried about our future. As part of the restructuring we had to keep diaries of our day-to-day work. In addition we all had interviews, which was like applying for a new job. As a team, we had to make a presentation about the live donation programme and the importance of this to patients and other service providers.

While the restructuring was ongoing, I and the team were put under enormous stress as the fear of losing our jobs was unimaginable. It was made harder by having to carry out our daily work at the same time. I applied for counselling sessions in order to cope. Morale within the team was low and the working environment unpleasant. It tested the relationships within the team and staff showed their true colours. The lead consultant was partly involved in the restructuring which I considered appalling as it seemed to demonstrate a lack of professional integrity.

Personally, this was made even more difficult for me as we were trying to move house at the same time. We were at the completion stage, by which time mortgage applications had been approved and paid. The survey report had been received as well as all the necessary legal work. You can imagine how excited I and my family were finally to be able to move after two years of house hunting during which time some potential purchases had fallen through.

However, due to the circumstances at work, we had to pull out, losing both the chance to move to a bigger property and our buyer who did not want to wait until we found another house to buy. We did not want to wait until my work situation was clarified, so we once again started looking for properties and for a new buyer of ours. It was a heart-breaking situation for me, but I put my trust in God that things happen for a reason and that the situation would work out in the end.

In England, moving house is quite a difficult process. You need to sell your property at the same time as buying another, so you are part of a property 'ladder'. If the buyer of your property needs a mortgage they can only do so once they have obtained one. It is easier for first-time buyers who do not have a property to sell and for cash buyers who do not need a mortgage. If you wanted to purchase a buy-to-let property, you would not have your own property to sell, although your vendor may need a mortgage to buy their next property.

We finally moved house and sold our flat at the end of 2013. With God's help, the house we are now living in was the best of all the properties we saw. The suburban location was ideal: it was like living in the countryside but close to the centre of London and was near the secondary school attended by my children. This was all part of God's plan and I have learned to be patient as God will eventually listen to our prayers.

Everything that has happened to me has happened for a good reason.

Meanwhile, at work, management had decided to half the number of staff in our team. This meant there were only two full-time members and me, who was still working part time. The position of recipient coordinator had been removed, so the work had to be taken on by the live donor coordinators. I was both sad and happy: sad that I had lost some members of my team, although they had been given a generous redundancy package; happy that I still had a job thanks to God and my Unison union representative. Having said that, could I be happy facing the challenge of running a service with very limited resources? I put my trust in God, however, who never gave me a task I could not carry out. Life and work had to carry on, whatever the circumstances. God always has a plan, however difficult things appear at the time.

Bullying, harassment, discrimination, and victimisation

How did all this start? A good question! I experienced bullying and racism from the lead nephrology consultant in the renal live donation team whose name I cannot mention for confidentiality reasons. My case formally began on 2 February 2020.

No healthcare professional working in a hospital should ever have to experience institutional bullying and racism. We are supposed to be saving lives rather than destroying the lives of colleagues. I am a whistle-blower because I could not tolerate this unacceptable behaviour that has occurred not once but three times.

How did it all start and why? I was born in the Philippines, and came to the UK in 2001 to work as a nurse to earn a living for a better future and to fulfil my vocation to help sick people. As a Filipino, my accent is quite distinct. In addition, I must think about what I am going to say before speaking, which annoyed my team, especially the lead nephrology consultant. I found her behaviour unacceptable from the very start of my role as a coordinator. She was unwelcoming and seemed to regard me with disgust. I later discovered that she had a Filipino maid, which may explain why she believed I was unsuitable for the role in which I was employed.

I did not really become aware of her initial reaction until I discovered later that she constantly intimidated me and found fault with everything I did, either in private or in front of my team. This generally happened every week and I just had to put up with it, although working with her was unpleasant. On the other hand, saving the lives of my patients gave me so much pleasure. I was not surprised by the comment of one of the admin staff who said, "I should have learnt to speak her language, then, perhaps, she will like me."

As the years went by, I dreaded working in such a toxic environment that compromised my moral values and applied, unsuccessfully, for numerous other vacancies. My colleagues criticised me unnecessarily for trivial matters, seemingly just to intimidate me. I felt bullied and harassed but kept quiet as I had to continue working with them. Their controlling behaviour was unbearable at times, especially when I returned from leave when they would criticise me for minor matters. In contrast, greater mistakes made by others seemed to pass unremarked.

As time passed, the situation seemed to become accepted as natural. I should have spoken up about it after my counselling sessions but one of the senior renal nurses told me not to complain. I was upset and felt vulnerable and should probably have been brave enough to speak out. But why was I encouraged not to? Is this the normal attitude for senior nurses to take, afraid to deal with situations which, as managers, they should deal with?

I was in the live donor team for eleven years and had three managers during this time. I spent two years on secondment as a recipient coordinator but moved back to my role as live donor coordinator after the 2013 restructuring. Although the role was challenging, saving lives was the icing on the cake, which is why I stayed in the role for such a long time. However, following the appointment of a new manager in 2015, I become hugely frustrated and disappointed and applied for a position as a Band 8 recipient coordinator in 2016.

I was very proud to have been offered an interview and visualised how I could develop the role to best serve my patients and the renal department in general. The plan I envisaged for the new role excited me tremendously as it gave me a chance to work without the controlling behaviour of my colleagues.

I had prepared thoroughly for the interview and had practised my presentations. I felt that the interview went well and was told that I would be informed of the outcome that same afternoon. However, I did not hear anything and the next day I was called into the office of the lead renal nurse who told me I had been unsuccessful. She explained that my communication was poor and that I was not ready for a Band 8 role due to recent events between me and my manager. These would be mentioned in my forthcoming appraisal.

I was shocked as I thought my interview had gone well and was puzzled by the mention of my appraisal. I was given further feedback that afternoon by the lead nephrology consultant who reiterated that my communication skills were poor and that she therefore had to clarify everything with my patients. I was shocked and confused by the feedback. I even hugged the senior renal nurse for support; this kind of feedback from her was unprecedented. She even told me that "if she had been the interviewer, she would never have hired me at all".

I felt sad and unbelievably sorry for myself, but I had to carry on doing my job that afternoon and put everything out of my mind as it was the live donor clinic. I had to move on and try to do my best. However, I began to encounter problems communicating with the patients, which was really surprising as I had never had issues with the Patient Advice Liaison Service (PALS) nor had complaints from patients during the six years in that role. Patients began complaining about missed appointments and the clarity of communication. These began to occur near the time of my appraisal.

When the day of my appraisal was approaching, I was told by my colleagues that someone wanted to get rid of me and that I should just submit to the appraisal feedback that I would receive from my manager. I was confused by this statement; I did not know what it meant until the actual appraisal took place. The appraisal is an annual performance review carried out for every employee, where your past successes and achievements are discussed, as well as your future career aspirations in order that a training programme can be put in place. During the discussion each individual achievement and your overall performance is scored, which must be agreed between you and your manager.

The annual appraisal is usually carried out in June or July. Although I had to prepare what I would say, the appraisals do not vary much from year to year. During my appraisal there was the normal informal discussion but, unusually, we did not score each of the tasks I had performed during the year. The scores range from exceeding expectations to underperformance. I was surprised when my manager told me that, overall, I had underperformed during the year — a huge contrast with what was my actual performance.

During my six years in the role and in my previous nursing career, I had been judged as either excellent or good during my appraisals, so this was the first time I was deemed to have underperformed. The reason given by my manager was that I did not do well in my May 2017 interview for a Band 8 role and that I had poor communication skills. I was shocked and could not believe what I was hearing, although after my interview I had been told that this feedback would be brought up at my appraisal.

Why was this fair when I was working so hard to look after my patients in an understaffed team due to colleagues on long-term sick leave for months and in which the manager was not carrying out her role? It seemed bizarre that I was to be punished for attending an interview. My administrator told me it was my fault for applying for a Band 8 role. How could this be my fault?

I told my manager that I was not happy with my score and that it should be increased to good, at least. However, she requested that I accept my score as it could increase once I had attended a communication study day. I was unhappy with the way the appraisal had been conducted, which I considered absurd and unfair. I had performed exceedingly well, had communicated properly, had great teaching feedback, and had dealt with complex transplants for six years in the role.

My manager told me that I was to be put on an underperformance management review, after which I could be disciplined or even dismissed, so I should just agree with the score given me. This seemed like a joke. I was not agreeing with her because her assessment of my performance was wrong. But instead of correcting their mistakes, I was threatened with the underperformance review. How ridiculous was this?

I could not find information on how I could appeal against the appraisal so I asked a retired senior education nurse, who told me there was no appeal process available. I was shocked and wondered if what she said was correct. It was really frustrating but, eventually, someone in another department of the hospital told me that there was, in fact, a process in place through which I could question the outcome of my appraisal.

One weekend after my appraisal, a miracle happened. My washing machine had broken down so I had to go to the local laundrette. A stranger noticed that I was looking depressed and he advised that I go to church. I had no idea who this middle-aged man was or why he saw fit to offer me advice. However, as I felt so desperate I went to the home of Father Michael of our local church, which was not open at the time. He was shocked when he saw me looking so sad and asked me to wait in his library while he prepared his next service. In the library I came across a book with the title of 'Finding your Voice'.

As I read the introduction and back page I became more interested and I asked Father Michael if I could borrow it. As I started reading it on returning home I realised that my prayers had been answered and that I would follow the advice in the book and speak out, whatever the situation, in order to get what I deserved. I had found my voice and would not be silent!

I called my union for advice but needed to complete some forms before I could be given any. Furthermore, I had requested a meeting with my manager but this was not a success. She told me to agree to the conclusions of my appraisal so that they could be passed on to the lead nurse and my lead nephrology consultant, which I found bizarre. She told me that my appraisals would be better once I improved my communication skills, and that lots of patients had complained but she could not provide any evidence for this.

During the appeal process several confusing things happened. A patient of mine had not attended an appointment as someone had called him by telephone to cancel it. My manager blamed me for this despite me confirming the appointment with my patient. Another example was the day I called in to work explaining that I would be late as I was not feeling well. When I arrived I was told that I had been requested not to come in. There were also IT problems, such as missing emails, which had never occurred before my appraisal.

There was so much confusion during the time of my appeal that I had to take sick leave due to stress. My union was little help either. Once when I called, I could not understand what the man on the line was saying. Every time I reported him to the main office, I was told that there was no one who could help me except him. I found this unbelievable and received no support from the union in my time of need.

My mental health suffered immensely. Before taking sick leave, I was told by the counselling service that they did not have any near-term appointments available. Where were all the people who should have been there to help me? I had worked hard for many years helping numerous patients through the difficult transplant process as well as supporting the colleagues in my team. Throughout my career I had always helped ensure that the patients received an excellent service.

As I was suffering from depression and anxiety, I was given counselling and cognitive behavioural therapy as well as receiving support from my GP. I had never felt like such a failure in my life and was crying almost every day. My children were also affected by seeing me in such a state. I was pleading with the Lord to guide me as I didn't know how to get back on my feet in these extremely difficult times.

While I was on sick leave I reflected on everything that had happened. I felt it was completely unjust and inhuman to use me politically in this way. My team were supposed to help but they had agreed with the allegations made against me about my poor communication skills. I could not believe that a human being could be capable of so much evil just to protect themselves when they found themselves in the mess caused by management. They were complicit in this terrible crime when they should have been doing what was morally right. I was caught up in a terrible mess and felt bullied and victimised.

While I was off sick, I realised who my true friends were. Some of my work colleagues, who I thought were friends, disappeared as they feared retribution from work by associating with me. My genuine friends were always on hand to check how I was doing. I was fortunate that I always had someone to accompany me on a walk, for example. I have listed all the friends who helped me in my acknowledgements. One of them was Cecille Gubatanga, who was a walking buddy and great company.

I was on sick leave for three months and, due to my absence, no progress could be made on my case, which seemed bizarre. I requested that I make a grievance claim against my consultant but was not allowed — because she was a consultant, an explanation I found odd at the time. Later, while on leave, I finally managed to meet my union representative and was hopeful that I would be able to bring my grievance claim.

How was this episode resolved? Would I go back to work despite my lack of trust? It felt like a marriage separation: would you go back to your partner after all the backstabbing and mistrust? After CBT, talking therapy, and counselling from an independent advisor, I agreed to have mediation with my manager. The consequence was that my appraisal score was increased to good by the lead renal nurse. I decided to return to work. And why not? I was not at fault and loved my job more than my manager did, who I felt had totally messed up by following an order from higher up.

As a nurse, I thought we should always be vocal in bringing to light any wrongdoing. Why then did my manager follow an order when it was the wrong thing to do? During mediation I was told that the decision had been made by management and that my interview for the Band 8 position would be mentioned at my appraisal. As a nurse, or as a moral human being generally, are we not supposed to oppose a wrongdoing rather than support it? Should you carry out orders from your superiors even though you know them to be wrong?

In my opinion, my manager was wrong, and actions like this will lead to further damage in the future. In many ways, my work was a success as, with God's protection and guidance, I always did the right thing for my patients. I strongly believe that wrongdoing destroys reputations and will always be exposed in the end as the truth is revealed, so why not be honest and kind from the start? What is wrong with society nowadays? There seems to be a culture of lies and deceit, an abuse of power, at the expense of others.

After mediation, the relationship with my manager and team improved a little and I felt more settled. But I still could not stop thinking about what had happened. On my return I was surprised that none of my team had bothered to wash the cup that had been sitting on my desk for months. The unit did not seem to be functioning well as we rarely had any transplants booked and we were in the bottom three or four units in the UK performance-wise. I returned with what I thought was a clean slate but things soon deteriorated again.

My manager once again became a frustration, and I was sickened by the way that the lead consultant was forever covering her mistakes to protect her, which was unacceptable and never reported. It was frustrating and humiliating as I sometimes had to pick up the pieces in, for example, our follow-up service. There was a big question mark regarding my manager's performance. More annoying was the fact that she blamed others rather than take responsibility herself.

A few months later my manager went on sick leave and we later discovered that she had left the trust after battling with work issues. Soon after, the lead nephrology consultant also took sick leave for a few months. Our new manager was the consultant nurse. She was lucky to have been given the post as she had no experience of the roles of either donor or recipient coordinator. Two highly experienced senior clinical nurses were therefore to be supervised by this consultant nurse. Thankfully, for me and the rest of the team, we had survived in the absence of a manager on several occasions.

Things improved during this period. It was really noticeable that the lead nephrology consultant became much more careful while the manager was on sick leave. I wonder why? The period after she too took sick leave was the most relaxed and pleasant of my life. There was no pressure on me and we did not suffer the frustrations of having to deal with an indecisive consultant; there was no one to blame me for mistakes she should have taken responsibility for; and there was no overwhelming atmosphere of bullying and intimidation. Meetings were structured better, which made us more efficient, and there was now little negativity within the team.

But of course, it was natural that I should wonder why the consultant had taken sick leave. No reason had been given except for stress. After about four months, she suddenly returned to work, came into our office, and apologised to me. Her colleagues joined her and encouraged her to come back and work with us, so she was soon back as one of the nephrology consultants on the live donation team. I was advised that I could discuss clinical matters with another consultant if necessary, rather than her. In any case, she was apparently no longer our lead nephrology consultant.

Along with the rest of the team, I welcomed her back and she was soon carrying out her full workload. However, she still had an unprofessional attitude towards me. The paired and pooled patients' case reviews were complex and I was intimidated by the way she commented on my preparations for these. As always, I prepared well, but she intimidated me in front of the team, which I found unacceptable.

Issues arose when meetings were arranged in her absence. It was my understanding that she was not the lead nephrology consultant for the live donor team and yet she acted like a primadonna, complaining that decisions had been taken without her when she was unable to attend the multi-disciplinary meetings. Worse, management did not have the courage to stand up to her. One day she told me to apply for a new role as, apparently, there was something unpleasant happening in the unit. I applied for a Band 8 position in the renal transplant team as I felt that, once again, I would be the target of her intimidation, and that I would receive no support from management. Unfortunately, I was unsuccessful as before.

My feeling was that there was something bizarre happening at work and I explained this to my manager. I was fed up working with the consultant as I could not please her, whatever I did. Bullying also seemed to be indirect. For example, I would receive emails about patients complaining about me, as happened when I was disagreeing with my appraisal score. I knew what institutional racism felt like, and I was experiencing it once again. Although I felt anxious and helpless, there seemed to be no option but to carry on with my work.

I later received an unpleasant email from my consultant ML criticising my work. Although Filipinos are resilient, having had to deal with many hardships, I felt I could not tolerate this treatment anymore. My work has always been challenging, especially when we were short-staffed due to long-term sickness. For long periods of time, I had to work on my own to keep the service going: even though this was stressful, it was the work I loved to do. But stress caused by bullying and institutional racism was a different matter. It was traumatic and easily triggered.

Because I raised a concern about my work situation, I was being bullied and victimised again: the story of my life. The lack of compassion shown in how the situation was being dealt with was inhuman. As healthcare professionals, we should adhere to our code of conduct but this seems to have gone out of the window. Unfortunately, no one was brave enough to deal with the issues, and so the behaviour became accepted and rampant.

I decided to make a formal complaint as I could not tolerate the treatment of the consultant towards me. I wanted to put a stop to her behaviour and make her responsible for her actions.

I had been in my role for ten years and it wasn't in my nature to complain but I found the courage to do so as I thought I had little choice given that management did not intervene.

Despite what happened in 2017, I came back to work after my sick leave with a clean slate and forgave everyone. Nevertheless, the consultant's attitude did not change when she returned and I felt she would do everything she could to get me out of the way. This was evidenced by her most recent actions. Was I the reason she had been on sick leave for such a long time? Why blame me when it was her fault? The situation was unbelievable and made me realise what an unpleasant person she was. In summary, I found her a racist, a bully, and a coward for not taking responsibility for her actions.

I wondered how she treated her nanny at home who was a Filipina like me. If she can pinch the ear of one of the junior doctors, as was witnessed, what could she have done to her nanny in the privacy of her home? Why was she allowed to be a teaching consultant when she intimidated junior doctors? I knew of someone who broke down in tears because of the way she treated him. She had shattered his confidence and he had little choice whatever he did. If he left, her poor reference would make it difficult finding another job; if he stayed, he was stuck with a racist mentor. It was a unique experience working with such a manipulative and selfish control freak as her.

My formal complaint was not welcomed. I was being continually harassed to meet and discuss mediation. But I thought they were trying to brainwash me into accepting mediation so that they could then wash their hands of the problem. My manager only pretended to help me and was unkeen to give support during these difficult times.

Moreover, my manager was part of the bureaucracy that always sides with management. She was a coward who could not stand up for herself and do the right thing; matters were always dealt with behind the scenes. This was the type of leader in organisations that make for a toxic workplace and no real change will happen if the system remains the same. In addition, as I have mentioned before, no one liked dealing with painful issues like this; but they should never have occurred if they had been confronted at an early stage before they became toxic and irreparable.

My manager and I could not agree on a solution as she wanted to sweep the problem under the carpet. It was suggested that my consultant apologise to me. However, she had already done this, to little effect. I had also found mediation to be completely ineffective as it did not change her attitude towards me. What was the point of all these procedures to deal with matters of bullying and harassment? It seemed to me that their real purpose was merely to serve the management.

Other colleagues made mistakes but no one was penalised with poor feedback as I was. I was also penalised for attending university every Thursday because the unit was short of staff. I felt that I had to support and please them in everything I did; and if I didn't do this they would make my life hell by their control freakery. By studying for my master's degree I would be seen as more qualified than my colleagues which seemed to be why I should stop studying.

The explanation for these events was never given as the truth was swept under the carpet. If no one was listening to me, what could I do? Would anyone else have put up with this and let bullies control their life? If management can't help, what can one do? Do you leave and find a new job? Just quit and appear a total loser? Complain and hope that you will be listened to?

In my case, I could not find another job and so I found the courage to speak out and persist with my formal complaint. I also requested a secondment or redeployment but this was declined. I suffered a great deal mentally in 2017 and could not tolerate further intentional victimisation which was destroying me.

However, my worst nightmare became reality as I was confronted with the same victimisation as I had suffered in 2017. It seemed as though I was being deliberately confused and made crazy in order to make me question what was real and what was not. That is how bad this strategy of victimisation was. But the second time around, I knew the methods and was therefore better prepared to deal with them. In one case, I was told that I was distressed in a particular work situation while, in fact, I was calm. The colleague who accused me was herself distressed rather than me, but I was ignored when I raised this with my manager.

My formal complaint was raised in February 2020 with the head of the renal department and I expected that it would be dealt with promptly. I also had the support of my union. However, I felt my case was not taken seriously as it was referred back to the manager against whom I lodged the complaint, rather than someone independent. Therefore, there was a conflict of interest.

The whole situation seemed absurd but my union did not support me, so I had to play along despite my concerns regarding the conflict of interest. An investigatory meeting was arranged but I cancelled this at the last minute after speaking to my union representative. He said that he would speak to another senior nurse rather than the head of the renal department. However, for some reason, this did not happen so I was left to speak to my manager to reschedule the meeting with another investigatory officer. She instructed me to inform my union to prepare for the next meeting.

Due to the Covid lockdown, this investigatory meeting never took place and our programme was closed as it was deemed non-urgent. Everyone was temporarily deployed to emergency and essential services and I was sent to the haemodialysis centre at one of the satellite units. However, due to the recent condition of my husband, I could not work there and helped as much as I could remotely from home instead. The transplantation was put on hold until the Covid situation improved.

I was told to prepare the documents for all the patients in our transplant programme, in order to identify the number of pairs who were either ready for transplant, on work-up, or were having preliminary tests. It was a task I was able to do given my ten years of experience in this area. However, I was told to return to work rather than work from home, but I later discovered that my colleagues were allowed to work from home doing the same job of collating information as me. Confusingly, I was then told to isolate at home as I was working in a private hospital. The instructions seemed to change on a daily basis, which was put down to the Covid situation. In theory, therefore, it seemed that management could do what they wanted to suit their plan of deceit: it was one rule for them, one rule for others. The confusion could cover up the truth of their wrongdoing, which they were too cowardly to admit.

Moreover, I had an upsetting discussion with my manager about the work I was doing. I had collated all the information and handed it over to the head of transplants who was happy to present the data on my behalf to the nephrology consultant about whom I had lodged my formal complaint. However, we negotiated that I could participate in the meeting remotely without video. Despite following my manager's order to meet virtually, I was accused of not participating and threatened with redeployment or sabbatical leave.

This was one of the first allegations against me since the start of my grievance procedure and the first attempt to get rid of me by transfer to another department. During this time, I received a surprising email informing me that my complaint had not been upheld, that we should try to improve matters via mediation, and that I should take a leadership course. This was rubbish since I had not even received a date for the investigatory meeting.

My union was completely useless too. First, I was told to wait to proceed with my case due to the pandemic; second, that they couldn't help me as I had refused their suggestion for mediation; third, why would I pursue my complaint when the consultant said she would apologise? This was strange as the union knew nothing of the plan for my consultant to apologise; nor was there anything in the policy that stated that the grievance process would collapse in the absence of mediation.

I felt as if I was being given the runaround to make me feel like a fool and humiliated. Again, I felt as though I had been stabbed in the back and victimised physically and mentally. This was unforgivable as the actions appeared to have been done on purpose to make me suffer. I would rather be shot dead than be subject to a long period of torture at the hands of these people.

I had the courage to stand up to them, however, and I made an appeal that the investigations be reopened and carried out by someone other than my manager. In the meantime, I returned to work to carry out my normal duties. Immediately on my return, however, I was harassed by my manager for a meeting to discuss the work rules she had drawn up for our team. I had returned to work despite her persistent bullying and found that I had been redeployed to the track and trace team for three to six months without my approval.

Despite the trauma of harassment, I agreed to meet the manager to discuss the new workplace rules for the live donor team, which included a requirement that all the team be communicated with openly. Of course, I had much to say about why these rule changes had suddenly been made. In the interests of transparency, I requested minutes of the meeting. To my surprise, however, this was treated as a misconduct issue. What a deceitful way to treat me!

I was completely heartbroken as I had never had such allegations made against me in my entire 23-year nursing career. I have always followed the code of conduct and been honest and polite. It was totally unfair as I had witnessed other colleagues being unprofessional at work, including making racist comments, and although my manager was aware of these she never took any action. But suddenly, accusations were being made against me.

At the same time as this, the renal manager had partially approved my appeal and allowed the investigation to be reopened, but with no new investigatory manager. This was still to be my manager. How completely absurd was that? This time around I had engaged a solicitor to deal with my case as I had fallen out with the union representative who I had used before.

We sent an email setting out the potential breaches of my human rights in that I had not been given the right to appeal against an investigation that had been conducted incorrectly.

Management had seemed to deal with my case completely unfairly. However, I had no other choice but to take my solicitor's advice that we should agree to use my manager as investigator, as this would allow my case to be reopened. The decision upset me but I was told it was the only way forward; otherwise, the case would be postponed for a long time as my grievance would have had to be put before the head renal manager before it could proceed.

The whole process seemed like a joke and I knew that something was not right. The shortcoming seemed to be that the process served to benefit management rather than the person making the complaint. Managers could report nurses to the NMC without due process. This was unfair! My point was that things only happened if management agreed. Unfair!

I was told that the changes made pre-Covid were no longer applicable for some reason. There was no support at my hospital for someone like me who raised concerns with management. This made my work impossible even though I tried my best. It was wrong that all the practices that were acceptable pre-Covid were suddenly not. There was no flexibility when it came to the changes made for me. This was totally unfair!

The worst aspect was that my new colleague sided with management on this in order to avoid repercussions against her. She was a coward who said she would only support me if she didn't have to work with the consultant against whom I made my grievance complaint. This just highlighted the politics being played, and showed cowardice and poor leadership rather than dignity. I was upset by her decision and felt as though she had stabbed me in the back: I had liked working with her, mentored her while she underwent training, and welcomed her as a new member of the team. I felt let down by her actions, which just proved that she was one of the bureaucrats who only looked after themselves.

What selfish ambitions! How cowardly and undignified! During this time I realised that my colleagues were looking to get rid of me by passing on to management every possible mistake I made. They were aware that this would inflict pain on me, which was totally unacceptable! It was inhuman, there was no compassion, and they violated any expectations of trust. The worst thing was that, as healthcare professionals, these people should have adhered to the code of conduct, which required us to be trustworthy.

Let me continue with what happened next. My investigatory meeting was scheduled for July and my manager had arranged a preliminary meeting a few days before this to discuss the alleged misconduct issues. I found this inconsiderate, as the timing seemed intentionally to coincide with the investigatory meeting so that they would know what action they would take against me in the event that the case did not go as they wished. How smart! However, I knew what was happening and I hope that they will be forgiven when the day of judgement comes.

On top of all the pressure I was under regarding the investigatory meeting, my colleagues were also trying to confuse me in my daily work. It was incredible to see how they were trying to destroy my soul. These people were dealing with patients on a daily basis! How concerning! I wondered about the lies being told that were swept under the carpet. It was frightening to think about the extent of the deceit. There should be a public enquiry to investigate what was happening.

The worst aspect of the investigation was that the investigator was to obtain statements from all the witnesses, and that management was in control of these statements. This was why my manager had been given the job. From the start, I felt as if I was being manipulated due to my ignorance of the process and of my rights; advantage was being taken of my vulnerability and weakness. This was wrong!

The worst thing that happened during the grievance process was my suspension from work. This was as the result of a meeting I had with my manager when I disputed her unproven allegations against me. She burst into tears, left the meeting, and sent the lead renal nurse to deal with me instead. I was being harassed on a daily basis while carrying out my work by the lead nurse. Every day she summoned me for a meeting. She told me that, due to my health, there was a risk in me remaining at work and that patients had complained.

However, when I challenged her about these alleged complaints, I did not receive a clear answer. I told her that I was caring for patients and booking appointments and had not encountered any problems. I asked her to put all the allegations of complaints in writing but she refused to do so. She told me to take immediate annual leave but I refused, as I had already booked it for two weeks hence, so saw no need to bring it forward.

The daily meetings in my office with her continued and she told me that I was to be transferred to the Watford dialysis unit because of the risks involved in me remaining at my present unit. I found this unbelievable and unjustified. She said that one of the risks was that my current behaviour was different from before. This was correct as this time around I was standing up to the harassment and victimisation. However, when I told her about the behaviour of my colleagues, one of whom would shout unnecessarily, she was not interested. She was only concerned with my behaviour, which was unfair.

The last time she turned up at my office I refused to meet her as I was in the middle of work. However, she refused to go away and blocked the door so I could not leave. This prompted me to call the police as I felt scared. She did then leave my office but called the deputy of nursing as a back up. The worst aspect of this was that she failed to acknowledge my emotions and conducted the conversation in a corridor where it could be heard by other members of staff. This was totally unacceptable and inappropriate behaviour by a lead nurse.

I sent her an email requesting that all the allegations against me be put in writing. I was then disconnected from the IT system, meaning that I had no access to email. Despite this, I turned up for work the next morning but could not find my card which gave access to patients' records. The next thing I knew, my colleagues left the office and the lead nurse entered with my letter of suspension. I remained calm, asked her what was going on, and called my solicitor. However, a security guard suddenly appeared and I was told to leave the office immediately, and was even asked why I needed to check the contents of my drawer twice. As advised by my solicitor, I accepted the letter of suspension, handed in my hospital identity card, said goodbye and God Bless You, and was finally escorted out of the building by a security guard. I felt sickened by the way I had been harassed by these people.

I later discovered that the letter of suspension alleged that I was unfit for work and at risk to myself and others, which was completely untrue. Why was I allowed to drive home or go by public transport if I was a risk to myself? Shouldn't they have sent me to A&E or sent a psychiatrist to assess me straight away? If they deemed me mentally unfit, they had a duty to protect me from harm. Their behaviour was totally unfair and unjustifiable; the people against whom action should have been taken were left untouched!

I saw my GP immediately as I was not going to be wrongly accused of putting patients in danger. If necessary, I would be the one who asked for help. I was judged fit to work by the occupational health unit at work but also needed feedback from my GP. While waiting for this, I was told that the outcome of my investigatory meeting was to be put on hold until I returned to work. This was a change from the original plan for the outcome to be given by the end of August or early September; another instance of the games being played to delay the decision of the meeting. Totally unbelievable!

One of the themes I encountered during the grievance process was the discrepancies between the statements submitted and the minutes that had been taken of meetings. When I asked for a record of our conversations, they refused. Why?! They always had something to hide. Deceit, fabrications, intimidation, discrimination were all strategies employed to try and stop me from complaining. However, when I didn't, they continued to punish me.

I was viewed as a disease that must be eliminated rather than someone to be supported. Various policies on whistleblowing, 50/50 behaviour, and performance appraisal had been introduced, which looked fine on paper but were useless when faced with tackling behavioural issues in the workplace. The policies seemed to apply only to managers who wanted to get rid of an employee like me against whom false accusations had been made. It will be worrying for other staff in my position with no support system and who would be destined to lose out. I say this because the tactics employed by the team were constant victimisation and pressure; if someone weak were subject to this, they wouldn't last a week.

In my case, with thanks to God, I had people around me who gave me the courage, resilience, and faith to carry on. Although the third time around was not easy, I had mastered the strategy and was never afraid to speak out against those who should have taken responsibility. They should not be able to get away with what they had done and I didn't want them to victimise others. Their actions had long-term effects and were clearly intended to destroy a person's soul.

After being suspended for some time, I apparently needed another occupational health assessment to discover whether I was fit to receive the outcome of the investigatory meeting. Really?! I was being criticised for not being able to communicate verbally, yet they were happy for me to attend a meeting that was minuted. And I was deemed unfit to receive an email of the outcome of the investigatory meeting. I found their actions totally deceitful.

I told them that waiting for the outcome was stressful but, rather than showing compassion, I was completely ignored. I would have expected them to have some concern for my mental health and that my grievance would be dealt with as a matter of urgency according to the procedural rules.

I attended the OH meeting with my manager and the HR representatives and I was considered fit enough to receive the grievance report. The next day I received minutes of the meeting stating that I had agreed to be redeployed to the Watford dialysis unit. This was a complete lie and the third attempt to transfer me to another unit. The outcome of the investigatory meeting was that my grievance appeal had not been upheld. I was totally disappointed and felt as if I was wasting my breath; it was like hitting a brick wall. The worst aspect of the outcome were the lies in the witness statement, which were not corroborated by my colleagues. Given their unprofessional attitude, I was not surprised by the outcome. The investigation was conducted improperly and the analysis was incomplete. In addition, no evidence had been received from my GP, counselling, or OH. Therefore, I decided to appeal against the decision. This was submitted to the head of HR and copied to my local MP before the deadline of 22 December 2020.

In parallel with these events in December, I had a meeting with HR, my manager, and OH to discuss the final letter and my redeployment to the Watford renal unit. I was meant to be back at work in December but I decided to take a month's leave because of the situation at home, but my manager was not pleased. I was given authorised leave but I discovered that I wouldn't be paid despite having so much leave left to take. Worse, the two weeks holiday I took in August when I was actually suspended was not added back to my annual holiday allowance. This meant I was penalised financially and only received £400 salary.

In January 2021 I was supposed to meet my manager to discuss the risk self-assessment I had completed as part of the OH procedure before I returned to work. However, according to health and safety regulations, since I had raised concerns about my manager it was inappropriate for her to conduct the meeting. Although this was the correct procedure, it meant that the meeting was delayed while I waited for a response from HR.

However, any potential meeting was superseded by the news that the transplant programme would be postponed due to an increase in the number of coronavirus infections. Unbelievably, my manager was still trying to deploy me to Watford on the scheduled date for my return to work. Once again I took unauthorised unpaid leave as I refused to be redeployed to Watford given that OH had not recommended this.

However, due to the closure of the transplant programme, I had to be allocated to another workplace. The only options given to me were Watford, other renal wards, and ITU. None of these were suitable given my husband's situation. Once again, my manager was not supportive as I was standing up to her. After the meeting she was forced to give my details to the redeployment team to arrange a suitable workplace for me.

I was not being paid while I was looking for another opportunity. I completely understand the need for healthcare professionals to be on the front line during the pandemic but it was also important for me to prioritise my family's health. All my career, I had worked hard to look after my patients but I was unable to do so now because of the risk. I found it ridiculous and lacking in compassion that I, as one nurse among many, should have been asked to work. But I would have taken the risk myself if it wasn't for my family. This is just a way of telling you that support was not there when needed, especially for staff like me who had raised concerns against management.

Finally, I found an opportunity working remotely at a call centre for the booking of vaccinations, which I found exciting. In addition to the hour of training I was given, I also practised with my husband. I was told that staff could carry out their role after just a few hours training. However, I was not comfortable doing a job without being fully competent, hence the additional hours I put in.

At the same time as this, I attended an appeal meeting with my manager, an HR officer, and a deputy nurse, who was the allocated investigator. We went over what had happened and why I felt discriminated against. I burst into tears when I saw my manager who had constantly hurt me and lacked any concern about my well-being. I remembered the time when she was a good person, before she became cruel and bureaucratic, and realised that it had been wrong of me to trust her. She had manipulated me in order to further her selfish career ambitions.

I was told that it would be a week before the outcome of the appeal was released. A day before the release, I was informed that it would be fine to receive this via email, although in the interests of a good future relationship it may be better to meet in person. However, given my previous experience, I did not believe this. What relationship we had had been destroyed and I no longer had any confidence in them. Despite this, I was hopeful that justice would be done as my grievance had been dealt with outside the renal department.

However, my hopes were not fulfilled. The outcome of my grievance complaint was no different from the one I received in December. It just showed that no proper investigation nor any critical analysis had been carried out. The past year had been a complete waste of time, money, and effort. The investigators were not good enough and the outcome of the interview was inconclusive. Moreover, another procedural breach had taken place in that it took too long to set up the date of the meeting and investigations.

Returning to my work at the call centre, one week I was only able to work a couple of half-days due to technical problems. The call centre manager took me off my position as, apparently, I was not meeting my target after just one day on the job. Despite my plea to remain and a request for further training, I was told that I was unsuited for the role. In fairness to me, the job was not straightforward as the script required further clarifications regarding privacy and clinical governance issues. However, my concerns were dismissed by the manager who had little time to deal with my questions. I was told to speak to my former manager (who had retired) or the lead nurse who had suspended me in August 2020.

I therefore emailed the lead nurse to tell her I was looking for more suitable work. She replied that she would still like me to work at a renal satellite unit or on another renal ward. But I told her that these solutions had been discussed many times with my previous manager and that we had agreed that I work in the vaccination call centre. Despite these explanations, I was given another disciplinary warning on account of the tone of my email and because I had informed HR of her inappropriate behaviour.

I took my concerns to my solicitor who was to engage a barrister to review my case before going to the tribunal. The process was a constant battle against stubborn people who would not admit their mistakes. I was told that no one in my position would ever win their case as the NHS feared damage to its reputation. There were so many events and people involved in my case that it was extremely difficult to untangle. But I strongly believe that truth will always come out in the end and that the NHS would be ashamed when it eventually did.

One of the issues was that because so many people were involved it became like a conspiracy against me. It seemed to be a deliberate tactic to make me understand and forgive them, otherwise they may lose their jobs if found guilty. But why victimise me in the first place? It seemed that I, among everyone involved, was the only one who would be disciplined.

The team of bullies appeared untouchable. It seemed acceptable that they could trample over someone like me who stood up to them and spoke out about the real facts of what happened. Someone once told me that no one wins by complaining at work, and that I should just ignore any concerns. I found this unfair! This is how inappropriate behaviour becomes accepted. I understand that workplace bullying happens every day, but the victimisation I suffered was a completely different scenario.

Later, the redeployment team placed me in a low-risk role in the finance unit at St Mary's Hospital. Although the trust was huge, this was apparently the only suitable vacancy they had for me. I worked within the hospital rather than at home, remotely. I was given training and support and the staff seemed kind and supportive. As a result, it did not take me long to adjust to my new role and work independently with little supervision.

Meanwhile, I discovered that the live donation unit was partially open and that my colleagues, including the consultant, were back at work seeing patients. Moreover, they had hired an agency nurse to help out, despite the pandemic. It was upsetting to have discovered this as I was told that the service had been closed and everyone had been redeployed to help with the pandemic.

I had already been bruised by my deceitful and unsupportive team who had stabbed me in the back and this new discovery just reinforced my view. I was sickened by the continued deceit which went unremarked. This was the last straw for me and completely destroyed my faith in my colleagues; they had proved to me they were unbelievable liars. You could argue I was wrong in this view but, for me, their behaviour was unacceptable. I expected that healthcare professionals should act with integrity and I could no longer tolerate this kind of behaviour from them.

At that time, I felt that I should just leave work altogether as there appeared little point in raising concerns when no one seemed to care. I enquired whether I had any grounds for constructive dismissal given that I had been in this situation for so long and no one seemed to care what was right or wrong. My meeting with the barrister had taken so long to arrange that, in the meantime, I received an email from the lead renal nurse stating my last day of work in the finance department and that I was to return to the renal unit. However, I could not go back given the pain I had suffered there. I therefore signed off as sick due to stress.

While I was on sick leave, I met my barrister. It was recommended that I return to work as this would put me in a stronger position. If things became unbearable again I should seek further advice from my solicitor. My best option then would be to seek permanent redeployment. This came as a shock to me as it seemed that no action was to be taken against management.

In addition, my discrimination case was not pursued as it was deemed impossible I would win. I felt very frustrated and depressed; all my efforts had been a waste of time and money. It just showed that there was no real justice when trying to fight the giant that was the NHS. I felt let down by the system, my solicitor, and barrister who were supposed to help me through this difficult time. I could not believe that such a system could have existed in the UK.

I was depressed by this surreal outcome. It was hard to comprehend that there was no justice for me because the corrupt system worked only for the bureaucrats. I did not stop pursuing my case and tried for a pro bono barrister only to discover that they could not help me. It took me three days to prepare all the documents but I was told I was not qualified for pro bono legal advice as I owned a house and could therefore withdraw equity to pay my legal expenses. I pleaded for help and explained the complexity of this case; if I had to sell my house to pay my legal expenses I would be homeless.

Despite the pleading, no one could help me as I felt they were all scared, perhaps. As a last resort, I contacted the Metropolitan Police, the BBC, and a *Guardian* journalist but had no luck as I was told that it wasn't in their area of interest or my emails went unreturned. My world had turned upside down and I felt bound in red tape and by a culture of cover up. The way my case had been dealt with was appalling and unacceptable. Even the Philippine Embassy could not help: in my opinion, due to fears of retribution.

My union also advised that I should no longer pursue the case as it was impossible I would win. This seemed unfair. The stress I had been under caused what was possibly irritable bowel syndrome, and my teeth had been damaged due to constant grinding. I had to wear a protective brace at night.

I am currently waiting for my counselling session which has been delayed due to the lack of counsellors. In addition, I am also waiting for my gastro referral appointment to check what is wrong with my stomach. Fighting the NHS — this giant god on earth — has caused physical and mental stress. My unexpected outcome was due to a failing justice system that covers up the powerful and discriminates against someone like me.

It was sickening to have witnessed and experienced all this; it was a world I did not dream about or live for. Rather, it was a completely messed up world run by corrupt people. I hardly recognised it and it was a failing on my part not to have realised this from the very beginning. However, you only become aware of reality once you have experienced it. The world is full of greedy people with selfish ambitions who act at the expense of others.

No wonder, then, that such behaviour has become accepted as the norm and is tolerated. Management seem to be able to do anything they like in order to be in the good books of their superiors by following orders, even when this was the wrong thing to do. They suffer no repercussions, even when they make mistakes that are accepted or covered up. You could even say that bribes were involved when mistakes were brushed under the carpet, and no one could speak out for fear of being accused of bribery. As a result, important issues like discrimination in the workplace are never brought to justice.

It is like an image of hell: a hell on earth where torture, persecutions, crimes, and injustices are commonplace. The leaders of society have no experience of such adversity and act like a protected species; they either do not know how to deal with these issues or they ignore and cover them up, as members of an untouchable group. They are the perfect example of bureaucrats.

God bless you all. I hope you receive forgiveness from God when the day of judgement comes!

Chapter 8

Cultural beliefs and traditions

Family holiday in the UK

I grew up in a small village in the Philippines and led a simple life as a child. Playing in the back yard in the mud and rain was sufficient for my happiness. When I was growing up, our family holiday was a day trip to the nearby beach, and/or a visit to relatives. However, this was very different to our family holidays in the UK and I must explain why.

Why is there a need for holidays? Is the money spent worth it? Well, it is important to have a break to reflect and to recharge the batteries now and then. For me, holidays greatly benefitted my physical and mental wellbeing. They provided new places to explore and enjoyable experiences. As I had a family, I shared these experiences with my husband and children.

Holidays are usually taken during the summer in England, between June and August, when the weather is generally warm and calm. Each family chooses the type of holiday they like. Living in a rich country, there is a large number of choices available. Holidays can be taken anywhere in the world, and by any means — flying, cruising, or driving — depending on the amount of money you are willing to spend. Holidays are the norm in the UK and everyone looks forward to them.

The peak summer season is always the most expensive time to go. Singles, retired people, or couples with no children or young children can go away at less expensive off-peak times. When I first came to the UK I could not understand why holidays seemed so important to people, why they were always talking about where they have been and where they would like to go next. This is also the case for young people, who want to see the world before settling down.

It seems that a round-the-world trip is a 'must-do' for young people: the need to enjoy life before marrying. But why? It seems to suggest that after marrying and having children, the fun stops. But is this true? In my opinion, family life is fun too, and you can still travel with your family, so why the rush?

One of the reasons why a couple cannot settle down and marry early is the need for a stable career and to save money to buy a property. But travelling is expensive, so why not take fewer holidays to save more money for a house? And how certain can we be about the stability of our career? Circumstances can change. Some women end up having children at a much later age; others find out too late the unbearable truth that they are unable to have them. Moreover, the risk of complications in pregnancy increases as you get older.

Even if you have a stable career, this can be affected by the need to take care of your children. Alternatively, you could continue your career but leave your children in the hands of a nanny, a nursery, or other childcare facilities. Each individual couple must make the choice most sensible for them. I hope that mothers don't suffer from post-natal depression when they realise that they are unable to cope with life having a new baby to look after. And I hope that everyone reading this realises that it is not about your life but the lives of your children. To bring a child into the world is a big responsibility; they must be taught about the goodness in themselves and in the rest of the world.

Returning to our holidays, as a family we visited Ireland about three times a year, as this is where my in-laws lived. We spent most Christmases and Easters there and bonded as a family. Our summer holiday was normally spent at a UK seaside resort. The most enjoyable time was when the children were growing up as they loved building sandcastles on the beach and swimming in the sea. We normally spent a week away in summer surrounded by beautiful countryside with opportunities for hiking. Accommodation could either be our own tent, caravans, self-catering apartments, or cottages with or without bed and breakfast facilities. Our children enjoyed a wide range of activities such as hiking, cycling, crabbing, fishing, boating, and generally just exploring the beautiful countryside.

Our family tent

God has given us the free will to decide what we want out of life. The only advice I would give is that you must take responsibility for your actions and accept the consequences of your mistakes. At the end of the day, we are all imperfect human beings. No one can hide from these mistakes and the truth will always be revealed eventually.

As for me and my family, we worked on our relationship. As we loved each other, we always found ways to resolve problems and to forgive and forget. We committed to an everlasting relationship. Therefore, it was not a matter of where we went on holiday or how expensive it was; the most important thing was that we enjoyed each other's company, and this made our holidays a worthwhile break.

Hiking, spending time on the beach, and children's activities while on holiday

Food, weather, diversity, culture, and traditional celebrations in the UK

This topic should be written about by someone born in the UK and who grew up with its beliefs and traditions. I did not. However, I am nevertheless able to compare my experience in the relatively wealthy UK with that of the Philippines, a developing country. I should consider myself privileged to have had such a background as part of my learning experience and growth. I am open, flexible, and adventurous and love to learn new things, such as discovering a wide range of different foods.

Living in the UK is one thing, but I also had a husband who was an Irish-born UK citizen. This gave me an advantage over a Filipina living in the UK who was married to a husband from the same culture. I had insight into both worlds which made me better able to understand and relate to situations. Having to balance between two different worlds in a respectful way meant having to embrace inclusivity and diversity.

I should begin by saying that one of the most basic facts of life to learn is that you should be open. I would not have been able to live with my husband without the ability to compromise. And one of the great ways I had to adapt was to learn how to cook traditional UK foods, which I generally enjoyed eating too.

In my household, we had three meals a day: breakfast, lunch, and dinner. Our breakfast was generally cereal or a traditional full English breakfast on some mornings. This consisted of eggs (scrambled, boiled, fried, or poached), sausage, bacon, mushrooms, tomatoes, and either black pudding or baked beans. This breakfast is often served in hotels and B&Bs with toast, coffee or tea, and fruit juice.

English breakfast

A popular light and quicker breakfast would be toast served with butter and jam or marmalade. There are many types of jam, such as strawberry or plum, and they are one of the delicacies in the UK. In past times, people would pick fruits to make their own jam. This is unsurprising given that many of the fruits used to make jam grow in the UK. These products are widely available in supermarkets.

Lunch will typically be a sandwich, either homemade or bought, and a drink: tea, coffee, or a soft drink. Sandwiches are made with white or wholemeal bread and can contain a wide variety of fillings: cheese, meat (e.g. chicken, beef, ham, sausage, bacon), salad (lettuce, tomatoes, cucumber), together with mayonnaise and/or salt and pepper. Sandwiches for vegetarians would not contain meat.

I make sandwiches for my children to take to school for lunch and, generally, my husband makes his own to take to work. I have sandwiches myself, but prefer something hot. Sandwiches may not satisfy my appetite as much, but they are convenient and easy to prepare. Marmite is a popular sandwich filling in the UK. I always have this in my cupboard, as one of my daughter's friends likes a marmite sandwich when she comes to visit.

Soup is also popular at lunch, again either homemade or bought. It is often eaten with bread and can be made from a wide variety of ingredients, such as chicken, peas, tomatoes, carrots, or other vegetables. It can be served as the starter to a three-course menu of starter, main course, and dessert.

Dinner is considered the favourite meal of the day. One of my favourite dinners to cook is roast chicken or beef, roast potatoes, steamed vegetables, and/or Yorkshire pudding and gravy. This is one of the easiest, but most sumptuous, meals to serve in the evening. Hot meals are preferred at this time after a long day at work.

Other traditional meals are pies (e.g. fish, steak and ale, cheese and onion, cottage, or shepherd's), beef or lamb stew, and fish and chips (on Fridays). In the UK, potatoes, rather than rice, are the major source of carbohydrates. Roast turkey is traditionally eaten at Christmas. Some vegetables I only discovered when I came to the UK include sprouts, parsnips, and swede. Herbs, such as parsley, are used to enhance the taste of the food. As London is one of the most diverse cities in the world, there is a wide variety of cuisines available in shops and restaurants.

At home we generally try and eat a variety of foods three times a day, but, unlike in the Philippines, we do not eat rice three times a day. Although I grew up with this habit, it is too heavy for me now. Heavy meals are necessary in the Philippines due to the working and living conditions.

In the UK, hot drinks such as tea and coffee are popular. This could be due to the cooler weather than in the Philippines, where people generally have cold drinks, especially during summer, to help keep the body temperature down. Afternoon teas are also popular in the UK, often served with scones and cream. This is especially the case in certain regions, such as Cornwall, where they are considered a local speciality and attract lots of tourists.

Desserts in the UK are a pleasure to eat and come in a wide variety: apple pie with or without ice cream, fruit crumbles, or cakes such as Victoria sponge, coffee and walnut, lemon drizzle, or banana. Christmas pudding is served as part of the Christmas meal. For supper, after the evening meal, and before going to bed, people may eat toast with or without milk, or cheese. Some may also drink wine, either to increase their appetite, to relax them, or just out of habit.

I may have forgotten some important things regarding food and drink in the UK but at least I have given you some insight. I admire those people who try and live and eat in the healthiest possible way. This is certainly the case for my husband and his family who try and follow a healthy balanced diet.

My next topic, therefore, is the importance of exercise. It is possible to participate in a variety of sports, either by joining a club or a gym. Running and cycling seem to be the most common, but every sport has its own club and you can participate as much or as little as you like.

However, some people like me prefer to walk or swim without joining a club. The advantage is that you have the flexibility to exercise when you choose; it does, however, require more self-discipline. For some people, sport can become a career. Inspired by successful sportsmen and women, they start playing, for example, football, cricket, or tennis in local leagues, before progressing to international competitions.

The weather played an important part in my decision in contrast to a country like the Philippines where the temperature can become so hot that walking is unbearable. UK weather is cool enough most of the time for walking or taking other exercises in a nearby park. One of the advantages of living in a wealthy country with excellent facilities is that the cost of gym membership is reasonable, in contrast to the Philippines.

My children have grown up with this lifestyle. From an early age they had huge opportunities to try new things, again, in contrast to a relatively poor country like the Philippines. If children in the UK demonstrate a talent at an early age they have the opportunity to develop this if they so desire. In the Philippines, it is much harder to develop your talent when only the rich can afford to use the facilities and resources necessary.

My point is that people in the UK are in the privileged position to be able to take advantage of the massive opportunities on offer. It comes down to a question of personal choice and whether you have the drive to take advantage of these opportunities. Do you take control of your life or leave it to chance? Or is it both?

One of the great things about living in the UK is the passion for the environment and love of nature. Everyone seems to do their best to save the planet via recycling, using alternative energy supplies, etc. There is also an amazing culture of volunteering whereby people give up their own time freely, without pay. This is one of the best qualities of the people living here.

One of the best examples of this was during the 2012 London Olympics, which would not have happened without the unselfish contribution of the volunteers to help at this once-in-a-lifetime event. More recently, the Covid vaccination centres have been generally staffed by volunteers. Without them, it would have been impossible to carry out the vaccination programme.

Younger people are given the opportunity to be part of this culture. The Scouts teach children to help make a difference to society. Teenagers have the opportunity to be part of the Duke of Edinburgh Award scheme during which they take part in worthwhile and rewarding community activities. One of the purposes of these awards is to shape communities for the better via this voluntary work.

Voluntary work is encouraged and supported in schools, churches, and charity shops. Retired people form voluntary organisations in order to spend their time more purposefully to help local communities. There are also good opportunities for lonely people to socialise and make new friends. The local park is a good example, which is maintained by volunteers.

Volunteers planting trees in one of the local parks

Moreover, there are fundraising events held throughout the country to raise money for charities such as for cancer or kidney research, or for helping vulnerable children. These events could take the form of sports such as fun runs, cycling, swimming, or sky-diving; or funds could be raised at simpler events like coffee mornings, cake sales, or shaving your head. There are large annual events such as Red Nose Day or the London Marathon where participants, international as well as local, can raise money for their favourite charities.

There are four seasons in the UK: spring, summer, autumn, and winter. Spring is from March to May, and is the time of year when the clocks go forward one hour. Everyone, including myself, looks forward to this season after the dull and cold winter. Nature comes back to life in spring: flowers blossom and leaves begin to appear on trees. Snowdrops are the first flowers to be seen, followed by daffodils and others. Cherry blossom is beautiful and gives people hope as they anticipate summer.

Garlic and tulip flowers blossom at the start of spring

Summer is from June to August and is the season when we expect the sunniest weather. It can be disappointing, however, as it is sometimes cooler than we hope. This is extremely frustrating for people like me who are desperate for a warm sunny day. As the weather can be so unpredictable, we have to be ready for anything and cannot put our coats away for summer in case we need them on cooler days. Therefore, we always pray that the weather for our annual family summer holiday is warm and sunny. On other occasions, we can experience heatwaves that last for days followed by thunderstorms and lightning. We have to be prepared for all this unpredictable weather.

Summer in the wilderness

Autumn is from September to October and is when temperatures start to drop. Leaves change colour during this season and trees everywhere — in woods, parks, and streets — are transformed into a magnificent display of natural beauty. This is also harvest season and the Harvest Festival is celebrated in churches.

Autumn pictures of trees

Winter is from November to February and this season is cold, dark, gloomy, rainy, and miserable. Some people suffer from depression due to the weather. Clocks are moved one hour backwards and sunset is around 4 pm and sunrise about 7 am. Sometimes it snows, which is one of the consolations for children as they can build snowmen, have snowball fights, and go ice skating. I used to love winter as I never experienced it like this in the Philippines. But as I have got older I find it more difficult to bear because of the long gloomy months and cold temperatures.

Winter season pictures

Christmas, New Year, and Easter are celebrated in the UK as they are in other countries. Christmas is traditionally spent with your family. Roast turkey, roast or mashed potatoes, and gravy is generally served, followed by Christmas pudding. The food can be accompanied by mulled wine or cold drinks, such as various fruit juices. Gifts are exchanged and the family plays board games. Families make a special effort to be together on these occasions.

Boxing Day is the day after Christmas Day. It was traditionally celebrated as an extra day's holiday for servants in rich English households in order that they could celebrate

Christmas with their families, given that they had to work on Christmas Day.

Spending time with the family at Christmas, and a Christmas wreath

Easter is given special emphasis in Christian churches as this is the time of Christ's resurrection. Some schools, especially primary schools, will celebrate Easter by an Easter parade when children wear homemade Easter bonnets. There are often Easter egg hunts, organised either by churches or individual families, when children hunt for hidden Easter eggs in competition with others.

Easter egg and an Easter bonnet

Other religions have their own celebrations, such as Ramadan, Eid, Baisakhi, Hanukkah or light festivals. Moreover, the UK has one of the longest lasting monarchies in the world and there are important royal events that are also celebrated throughout the UK, such as the Queen's Jubilee and Diamond Anniversary. Churches and local communities will gather together to celebrate with banners. In recent years, there have been several royal weddings, such as those of princes Harry and William. The latter was especially significant as William was the eldest son of Princess Diana and Prince Charles and therefore a future king of England. Huge crowds of excited people come along to watch and celebrate these occasions. Sometimes, as a treat, there is also a national holiday to mark the occasion, as was the case for Prince William's wedding. Traditional wedding dresses are worn; and for Scottish men, this could include kilts.

Photos of traditional Scottish wedding costumes

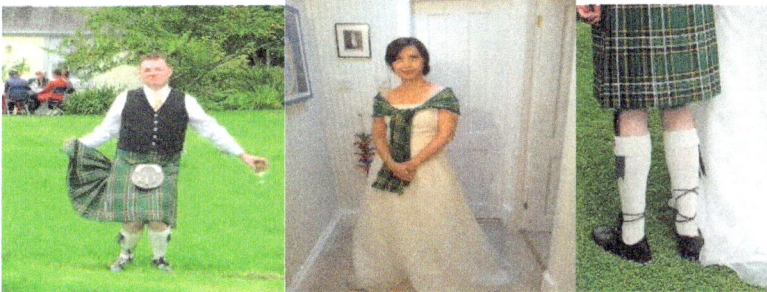

In addition to these national celebrations, there are also local events celebrated in specific communities, such as those where my sister-in-law lives, in Bonsall, a small village in Derbyshire. A farmers' festival is held there every year, organised by the local community. Farming vehicles are decked out with beautiful flowers and the villagers dress in traditional costumes. These events can last a week and people come to watch from nearby towns and villages.

Well-dressing and traditional games

During this celebration, all the villagers hang bunting outside their homes. Local artists showcase their arts and crafts in stalls. There is a well-dressing competition in which local wells are decorated with flowers and other items; there is morris dancing, game shows, entertainments put on by the local armed forces, a mini-market, and bars for eating and drinking. It is amazing for a visitor like me to feel part of the local community at this event.

Morris dance costumes

Other national celebrations include St George's Day, on which the patron saint of England is remembered, and Remembrance

Sunday. The latter is when those who died in past wars, such as World Wars One and Two, are honoured at huge events across the country. The day starts with a church service, followed by parades of the armed forces and local scout groups. Poppies and wreaths are laid at monuments in most villages, towns, and cities to mark the occasion.

One of the great annual celebrations for young people is Halloween. They dress up in traditional Halloween costume and have their faces painted. The children go from house to house playing Trick or Treat and are normally given a small treat, such as a chocolate. Churches may participate by holding Saints and Sausages evenings where children can carve pumpkins, take part in other arts and crafts activities, and play games.

Halloween costumes, and Saints and Sausages games

Guy Fawkes night is a celebration specific to Britain. It commemorates the day on which Guy Fawkes tried, unsuccessfully, to blow up Parliament. Since then, his failure is celebrated every year on 5 November with bonfires and fireworks, often held in local parks with crowds of people.

Music and shows are loved in the UK as demonstrated by the large attendances in smaller local halls or larger ones in the cities. There are tremendously talented classical musicians who practise endlessly to create beautiful music as members of orchestras, playing instruments such as flutes, trombones, string instruments, percussion, and piano. In addition to music concerts, there are also many theatrical performances to enjoy, especially in London's West End, and pantomimes at Christmas.

London is the largest and most magnificent city in the UK, and attracts many tourists from around the globe. The city is famous for its architecture, some of it dating back to Roman times. Well-known buildings include Westminster Abbey, St Paul's Cathedral, the Houses of Parliament, Buckingham

Palace, Kensington Palace, the Tower of London, and Tower Bridge. The London Underground is one of the greatest creations in the history of public transport. Its numerous lines, at various levels underground, take you anywhere in London.

Sketches of Westminster Abbey and a classic London street

Moreover, there is now a station from where you can travel under the English Channel by train to France, another example of a work of engineering genius to improve the transport system. Throughout the UK — in England, Scotland, Wales, and Northern Ireland — there are breathtaking natural landscapes, such as the Jurassic Coast in Dorset with fossils of dinosaurs tens of millions of years old.

Natural landscapes in the UK

England's heritage has also been preserved in its many historic buildings, gardens, and parks. Many ancient houses built of stone or with thatched roofs can still be seen. More modern houses are built of brick but these can still be beautiful and are one of the outstanding features of the UK housing stock. There are many art galleries and museums of various specialities to help present and future generations remember the past, emphasising the value of UK tradition and culture.

Thatched house of William Shakespeare

Chapter 9
Opportunities

UK Miss Philippines competition

Opportunities! A hugely important word for many of us! What is it? What does it mean? I have been fortunate to have had an amazing life and am thankful to have fulfilled all the dreams and aspirations I had as a child. I have received blessings from God, one of which was to have two wonderful children, Claire and John, who are the delight of our lives.

A traditional part of Filipino culture is the Miss Philippines beauty competition. I grew up with these competitions from a young age and beauty is celebrated everywhere in the Philippines. They were means of promoting and acknowledging beauty and competitions were held annually in every school classroom, as well as locally and regionally. The final goal was to compete in the national Miss Philippines contest.

This tradition has never been forgotten among the Filipino community in the UK. As a result, my daughter Claire was chosen to compete, with encouragement and persuasion from Philip de Vera. I never thought that Claire would take part in this; nevertheless, it was hard to ignore this once-in-a-lifetime opportunity as she had what it takes to win, and, after discussion with her family, she decided to participate.

The contestants for Miss Philippines UK 2019

I have no experience of beauty contests as I had never been selected to compete in the Philippines. Despite my sister and grandmothers on both sides of the family being beauty queens in our village, I was never interested as a child to get involved. I was therefore naïve about this world, although curious to learn something new. If you don't try you will never win, and a success for Claire would be a success for the whole family.

The rehearsal was long and tedious; discipline was needed in order to put on an amazing show on competition day. As a parent, I had to help provide the evening gowns, make-up, shoes, jewellery, etc. One of the elements of success was being able to be patient and endure all the preparations until the day of competition.

Competition day itself was a nerve-wracking experience, but, as a parent, I was also proud and excited to see my daughter on stage. I had never imagined she could look so gorgeous in the contest. It was very competitive, but Claire was brave and confident; she danced gracefully on stage and performed well in the question-and-answer section. She had both the brains and beauty to succeed and she excelled in every part of the competition.

The crowd cheered the candidates noisily, rang bells, and waved flags and banners. In addition, all the previous winners of Miss Philippines UK attended, as part of their duties. There were at least ten judges of the competition, all well-known people who had been selected on the basis of the contributions they had made to society.

I attended with my family and various friends. The announcement of the winner was a nerve-wracking experience, and my heart pounded when we heard that Claire was first runner-up for Miss Philippines and a winner of the evening gown award. Seeing my daughter's pride when she received the sash, flowers, and trophy was an unforgettable experience. It was a night to cherish.

Friends supporting Claire in her competition

What did we learn from this new experience? Claire and I both made genuine friends with the other candidates and their parents. From Claire's perspective, she gained additional knowledge of the traditions and culture of the Philippines. Moreover, she gained the confidence to perform in front of a crowd and to walk like a model.

The winner of Miss Philippines UK 2019

Miss World experience and modelling

The beauty pageant has given us a new perspective. As Keisha Quijano (who won Miss Philippines UK 2019) says in her statement below, beauty contests have the power to make a difference to people's lives. Claire and the other winners were constantly invited to events, such as meeting the Philippine Consul in the Philippines Embassy in London. She has taken part in photo shoots, newspaper articles, has had modelling opportunities, and has attended parties and events like Miss World.

Miss World and photograph with the candidate from the Philippines

One of the events Claire attended was London Fashion Week. It was amazing to see her experience this as a teenager. As parents, we were cautious as we had heard about the sexual exploitation of young girls by talent managers. However, we cannot keep Claire wrapped in cotton wool and she must learn to look after herself while knowing that we have given her all the necessary support. We pray to God every day for guidance in times of need for everyone in our family.

It is extremely hard for parents to let their children go, but it must be done as part of their education and development. One day, we, as parents, won't be here for them, so we must teach our children to be as independent as possible so they can grow and thrive as adults. However, Claire did not go to London Fashion Week alone; she was in the company of Keisha Quijano, an older and mature young woman who would not allow anyone to take advantage of them. I'm not saying that anyone would have done, but it was better to be safe than sorry.

The modelling was not as easy as one would expect as they had to practise their walks for weeks, wearing clothes from various brands. There were many far more experienced models present too, so they were in competition to best showcase their outfits. Claire wore many brands and was selected to model clothes from the greatest fashion designers during the week. She paraded on the catwalk with confidence and beauty and I watched her with great pride and joy. What this talented individual has achieved so early in life is amazing.

Claire in London Fashion Week and the Royalty modelling

Keisha Quijano's journey as she won the crown of Miss Philippines UK 2019

Why did you enter?

I was first introduced to the world of pageantry when I went to the hairdressers in the summer of 2019. I had never gone to the famous Philip de Vera before but on that day my usual hairdresser was closed. It was at Philip's, whilst getting a trim, that he said he could see me winning a pageant and that I should join Miss Philippines UK. At first, I thought he was either joking or just trying to make me feel good. I just tried to laugh it off and only understood how serious he was when he got me to read the application form and asked me for my number to send to the scouts. I cannot lie when I said I initially thought pageants were a joke. I naively thought the 'toddlers and tiaras' stereotype was the only truth and thought they were of no substance. Little did I know the extent and the limitless effort that really goes into it. To anyone who is currently of the opinion that beauty queens are 'airheads who are only in it for the glitz and glamour', I would like to raise the point that advocacies are a HUGE part of the bigger pageants (Miss World, Miss International, Miss Universe, Miss Earth, etc) and you can't enter without one. The point of the legitimate pageants is to show that you can be an AMBASSADOR of a brand and good cause. That is why we have a question-and-answer section about politics and the state of the world. There is a catwalk to show how you can capture a room in thirty seconds only and various media rounds to show how well you can engage GLOBALLY in this digital world. Having said that, I did not realise this during my haircut: it was more of a gradual learning curve throughout the whole process. In fact, at the end of my haircut, my only thought was 'why not? If anything, at least it will be a fun experience and I'll get to meet more Filipinos my age'. I personally love a bit of a challenge and a project to throw myself into, so this was the perfect opportunity to fill my summer with something fun and enjoyable.

How was your journey to winning the crown?
I had the most amazing time and winning the crown was the cherry on top of what was an already incredible cake. I was able to meet loads of amazing people who are now some of

my closest friends and I learnt a lot about myself. The weekly catwalk and dance rehearsals were gruelling but a lot of fun as we made it a good time by socialising and trying out new things. There were a lot of laughs and it never really felt like much of a competition as we were simply good friends having fun. It was more of a weekly meet up and dance session than a competition. Regarding the serious part of the rehearsals, I remember an interesting revelation I had when talking to some of the other girls about everyone's walking style and the general way they present themselves. YouTube videos promise to teach you how to walk but they only teach you the basics. Once you have mastered that then you can start playing with it and start personalising your walk and outfits to show the judges a more authentic version of you. It was so fascinating to see how everyone's personalities came through, whether in their outfits, their walks, their poses, or the way they talked in their introduction and question-and-answer section. I think it was at that moment when it sunk in that it does not really matter what others are doing or how they do things; that shouldn't really affect your performance. What matters is that we all had to show off who we were to the best of our ability and project our own self-love and self-confidence. The coronation night itself went by in a heartbeat. I have to say, it was manic: the quick changes, the hair and make-up, the dance routines. I remember the pre-start hug and 'good lucks' just before the curtain went up but before you know it, it is time to crown the winner. The night was great fun and to kind of come full circle, I was there to have the best time. I had prepped my heart out and practised the dances and walks at home so much that it became muscle memory so that I could just focus on having a good time and showing off to the judges who I am, giving them as much energy as I could. The crowd was the highlight for me. I distinctly remember the introduction portion. It was the time when you first go on stage to present yourself. For me, all the nerves and pre-stage shakes went away as soon as you heard the ROAR that came from the crowd. My support team came with banners, clappers, chants, and lights. I felt over-the-moon ecstatic, and cannot express how much the crowd carried me through. I am so blessed to have such great friends and supporters; I could not have done it without them.

What would you like to do to make a difference, having that title of a beauty queen winner?

It was a little way through the preparation process that I knew I wanted this for more than just the glitz and glamour of winning a crown and a title. The more I learnt about pageants the more I realised what their true objective is. Each pageant is centred around the ability to do good for your community. I feel that you can easily see through a girl that is just in it for herself and not for the betterment of those she represents — that was not what I was about or stood for. Once I won the crown, I set off to start something that I could build on to make a difference. Right now, I am working on 'FilBrit.ish', a platform and community I set up that promotes Filipino British businesses and talent. It is through this that I can meet and put a spotlight on so many great Pinoys in the UK and the fantastic work that they do. Throughout this competition, I learnt a lot more about my Filipino heritage and met so many people who were in the same situation as me. Many of us were born in the Philippines but had spent most of our life here. We know what life is like back in the Philippines and its mannerisms and culture but have not fully lived it. I heard a lot of similar stories of identity crises with people not feeling like they identify or belong solely in the 'British' category nor the 'Filipino' one. It was through this that I thought it would be a great idea to show that we are not alone, and that we belong to an incredible community of people with varying levels of feeling about this. Some of us have spent most of our life here, some have just moved, but we are all FilBrits and are making huge waves in our communities, flying our Filipino-British flag high. I want to promote the FilBrit community and their achievements through the creation of FilBrit.ish.

Any future plans?

Right now, I have just graduated from university and am blessed enough to have a job. In my spare time I am doing photo shoots and interviews to promote FilBrit.ish and the work I am doing with the MPUK team. I never expected to get into the media industry, so I have a lot to learn and I try to dive in where I can. My main goal and focus though is the growth and development of FilBrit.ish. The pandemic put a lot of things on hold (including plans to travel back to the Philippines) but it gave me a good reason to really sit and think about what I want my legacy to be. I am blessed enough to be able to hold the crown for another year and I plan to use this time to really promote Filipino-British culture as much as possible.

Instagram: @keishiaquijano

Chapter 10

Covid-19

Community response

Covid-19 began to appear in the local news in December 2019. It started in Wuhan, China and then spread around the world. The UK implemented its first lockdown in mid-March 2020 to slow the spread of the virus. The NHS was at full capacity, including Accident and Emergency (A&E) and Intensive Care Units (ICU). It has caused immeasurable deaths globally, a once-in-a-lifetime pandemic.

During lockdown we were not allowed to go outside except for exercise. Employees were advised to work from home unless this was impossible for essential key workers such as healthcare professionals or supermarket staff. Schools were closed, and lessons were conducted virtually. It was tough for everyone but especially for the vulnerable, or those with special needs or mental health problems.

No one in my generation had ever experienced such a pandemic. London, once busy, became a ghost town with hardly anyone on the streets. All hospitality venues were closed so there was no entertainment available. Even the airlines were operating at very limited capacity and only those passengers with a special reason to fly were allowed to.

London at the peak of pandemic

There were measures put in place to slow the spread of the virus. Face coverings in shops were mandatory and social distancing rules required that you had to keep two meters apart from others. Those who broke the law, such as not wearing a mask on public transport, were penalised.

Quiet London in Westminster

It was a life-changing experience. We had to communicate virtually with family members living elsewhere: not the best option, but the only one in the circumstances. New technologies were a great help but were a challenge to those, such as the elderly, who were not as tech-savvy as others.

The most severely affected group of people were the elderly. This group often had health comorbidities, which put them in danger if they caught the virus and so they were strictly advised to stay at home at the peak of the pandemic. People were classed as high-risk, vulnerable, and low-risk. The high-risk group included immuno-compromised people such as post-transplant patients or those undergoing cancer treatment.

Volunteers generously gave up their free time to help the vulnerable. The residents on our street became much closer, everyone giving a helping hand to those in need, or checking on them to make sure they were safe and sound.

Community response during the pandemic

People found innovative ways to carry on their work to maintain their mental health. Musicians, for example, started performing online. There was also a large increase in the amount of shopping done online. This continued even after the peak of the pandemic as some people were still cautious about shopping in-store. Many shops, especially clothes shops, have closed for good as their business has moved online. Although there was some government support, it was not sufficient for many businesses.

As a result, many people lost their jobs. The airline industry was the worst hit. To help, the government introduced a furlough scheme, whereby the salaries of employees of those businesses that successfully applied were paid by the government. This helped a lot of people survive financially but there were still many businesses that had to close despite this assistance.

The pandemic made people realise the irrelevance of money. No matter how much money you had, you could still catch the virus and maybe die. Expensive clothes and other personal items were irrelevant as there were no parties to attend where you could show these off. It made people realise that being with their loved ones was the important thing in life.

Parents had to stay at home with their children which was an unusual experience for those who went out to work. There were advantages and disadvantages to this. On the one hand, they could spend more time with their children rather than commuting to and from work. When schools reopened, it was also easier to send and collect them. On the other hand, some found it difficult to work and look after young children at the same time. A lack of social interaction with other adults was also a challenge for some.

The pandemic has devastated the lives of people across the world and killed many. It brought changes to the way we work and live. But it has also made us think about how to change our lives for the better. It emphasised the importance of being with our loved ones and the irrelevance of money in protecting us from the virus. It made us realise that money cannot buy happiness and love.

Nurse's experience

Covid response from our service

NHS hospitals and other healthcare providers such as GPs and nursing homes were hit hard by this unprecedented pandemic. There was a surge in patients awaiting admission to wards, while others were treated in A&E. There was a lack of capacity to admit patients suffering from Covid; ITUs were overflowing and some patients died. Non-emergency services such as outpatients' appointments and surgical procedures were suspended.

Our live donation programme was also suspended as we were deemed non-essential. It was not safe for renal patients to undergo transplants due to their vulnerability to infection; and there was no capacity to treat them due to the high numbers of Covid patients at the height of the pandemic.

The live donation programme resumed for a brief period once it was considered safe to proceed, although protocols for dealing with our patients changed. We had to carefully follow Covid guidelines such as adhering to social distancing rules, wearing face masks when required, washing hands, and using disinfectant. Staff were screened for Covid infection as part of these procedures.

In terms of patients, priority was given to those donors and recipients who were considered lower risk. Despite the resumption to our service, there were still various restrictions such as an inability to use donors from overseas. Transplant units in the UK and around the world shared best practices in order to conform to the new guidelines. For example, we screened both donor and recipient for Covid in the near final and pre-transplant stages. They were also advised to shield with the rest of their family for two weeks prior to the appointment and to report any Covid symptoms. We used the London Clinic as a pre-transplant and post-operation facility as part of the pan-London transplant collaboration.

It was a challenging time for everyone especially those patients awaiting a transplant. The team worked extremely hard to help those patients we could and, despite the difficult circumstances, we did manage to perform some transplants.

December 2020 saw the start of the nationwide vaccination program after the Pfizer and AstraZeneca vaccines were approved. Eventually, the aim was to vaccinate everyone in the UK. The roll-out started with the vaccination of healthcare professionals and key workers, followed by the most elderly and those people considered high-risk. Two doses were given to everyone ten to twelve weeks apart to give better protection. The programme was effective in that it reduced the mortality rate among the most vulnerable.

My first Covid vaccination details and the NHS patient information

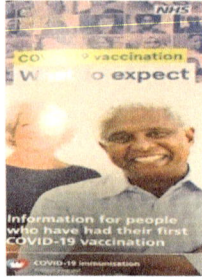

Since the pandemic started, the virus has mutated, producing several new variants. This was a challenge and research continues on the best ways to control or eradicate the virus. These new variants threaten to delay the return to a normal pre-pandemic existence. In the face of this uncertainty, there is a feeling of anxiety and hopelessness for many. In my opinion, the virus will be difficult to overcome even though some of the best scientists in the world are working on a solution. Covid will remain a challenge for everyone.

Healthcare workers resuscitating a patient suffered from Covid

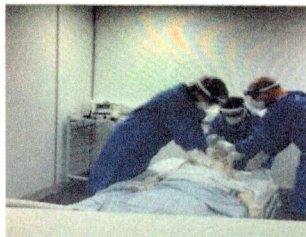

Nurse's experience

Staff nurse in the Intensive Care Unit at the Royal Free Hospital, London

The catastrophe brought by this terrifying pandemic is an absolute nightmare for all the healthcare workers and frontliners battling this contemporary crisis. As a nurse working overseas for the first time, it is even worse than you can imagine; all the uncertainties and trepidation were unbearable knowing that whilst I am facing this virus away from my family, friends, and loved ones, they are also in danger. In the last couple of months or more, hospitals have been like battlefields: wounded soldiers, fallen warriors of the modern era hit by the virus. I wrapped far more cadavers in this pandemic than at any time in the last five years working in the medical field, an event that I never thought I would experience, not even in this lifetime.

In the first surge, it felt like everything was consumed by darkness, with little knowledge of how the virus was transmitted or could be cured. I woke up each day, went to work, and wore my PPE with a little prayer hoping that we could save as many people as possible. However, it was never the case: every day we continued to count more casualties than recoveries. I felt that this hopeless fight was becoming routine. Countless times I heard families sobbing over the phone after hearing the passing of their loved ones. It was a tormenting time, but we never gave up as our patients were continually fighting for their lives and this spurred us on despite our broken morale and physical and mental exhaustion. Many of those who contracted the virus in the first wave were elderly, which reminded me of my grandparents. It was really heart breaking seeing them succumb to death unfairly without their family being able to bid their last goodbyes personally, with my hands holding their hands instead.

The second surge was even more overwhelming. People from all walks of life were admitted gasping and severely deteriorating, even those who were in their prime of life, with or without a past medical history. During this time, we had less support as redeployed and part-time staff who worked with us in the first wave had maybe chosen to stay at home or work at other hospitals. But we remained resilient and continued to work amidst the havoc ushered by this highly infectious virus. Things were clearer after the first surge: we had evidenced-based practice, supplies, equipment, and, most importantly, the vaccine. Somehow, we saw a ray of hope for the first time. I will never forget every time a patient was extubated or decannulated from their breathing tube as they headed towards constant recuperation. It was like a winning moment.

As I reminisce about those traumatic days, I also remember the tears I shed before and after every horrifying shift: the depression, anxiety, and all the negative emotions that most of us went through at some points were engraved in our minds and souls.

Nurse's experience

This is a story that was given to me by someone who worked as a paediatric nurse in one of the children's hospitals in the UK. We agreed to call her Daisy at her request to be completely anonymous.

Daisy has at least twenty years' nursing experience in the hospital. She spent her vocational career looking after ill children which was remarkable to me as I would prefer adult rather than paediatric nursing. She is married and has two young children. One of the children was considered as high-risk due to a genetic blood disorder. The other child is in good health. Her husband is a great father and husband, which makes the household secure: all in all, a happy family.

Daisy's husband is also a healthcare professional working in the same hospital. This was a great advantage in arranging shift patterns in order to best care for their children. As with all families, however, life is challenging at times, but it became worse when the husband contracted the virus and became ill.

Her husband worked in one of the Covid wards. The patients had a variety of symptoms but were generally coughing and needed oxygen to help them breath. Some patients recovered completely and were discharged; some developed post-Covid complications; some deteriorated and were moved to the ITU; and some, unfortunately, died.

As a healthcare professional, Daisy's husband had worn the correct personal protective equipment (PPE) when attending patients with Covid, in accordance with hospital guidelines. However, despite this, you could never be certain you wouldn't contract the virus. He commented that "It's dangerous to work in the hospital setting, one foot always in danger". All staff on that ward eventually caught the virus.

Daisy's husband routinely took a daily Covid test as part of the protocol and was shocked one day to discover that the test was positive. He was asymptomatic so was not suffering from a high temperature, continuous coughing, or loss of taste or smell, etc. He was instructed to go home and isolate. Two days later, he developed a high fever and diarrhoea; the day after, he lost his taste, and had a dry cough two days after that.

He was emotionally, psychologically, and physically affected by the virus, and had never before imagined that his life could be in danger. The thought of passing the virus on to the rest of his family, including his high-risk son, was unimaginable. What if it happened? It was something he would never be able to live with for the rest of his life.

The family had strict isolation and handwashing procedures to avoid passing the virus on to each other, not easy for a family living in the same household. Daisy had to enforce these strict rules on top of her normal chores and childcare responsibilities. She found it emotionally stressful because of the unknown consequences of contracting Covid.

Daisy's husband received the normal flu management regimes: drinking lots of fluid to keep him hydrated, and paracetamol to alleviate the pain and control his temperature. He ate at regular intervals, and had plenty of bedrest and sleep to build up his energy. After ten days, he began to recover. Thanks to God, he did not require hospitalisation or suffer further complications; nor did any other family member catch the virus.

Even though he still had a cough and felt tired, he went back to work after ten days at home. He did not require any further swab tests as per the protocol and returned to the Covid ward, hoping that he would not catch the virus again. His case shows the immeasurable risks taken by healthcare professionals, but they have little choice: life must continue as normal.

Nurse's experience
Marites Obtinario, A&E nurse in the Philippines

"Sometimes in life, we all need a hug. No words, No advice. Just a hug to make you feel better."

It has been more than a year, but I can still remember the anxiety when the Covid-19 virus started to invade the human body. It was 16 March 2020 when we got an order from the administration to immediately rearrange the Make-Shift Emergency Room set-up. At that time, we were handling an average of eighty patients in the ER (Emergency Room). I, together with my workmates, panicked: four Covid-positive patients would be coming in. Our available PPE equipment were surgical face masks, gloves, and alcohol: no N95, KN95, head cover, foot cover, isolation gowns etc. The only ventilation in the hospital was through large windows.

No Hepa filters, no area for donning and doffing, and there had been no plans to zone clean and dirty areas. Everybody was in panic mode including the patients, their relatives, and other healthcare workers such maintenance staff, security guards, and personnel gathering diagnostics (ECG, radio technicians, phlebotomists, etc.). It took us months to adjust to the situation. Protocols needed to change.

A lot of consultations were coordinated with the Hospital Infection Control Unit (HICU), Infectious Disease Service (IDS), Property and Supply Division (PSD), Pharmacy Department, Pulmonology, Radiology, and Anaesthesia. The Outpatient Department was closed. Scheduled operations were limited. Teleconsultations were the only means of communication with patients. Wards were transformed and divided into Covid and non-Covid wards only.

The schedules of nursing staff were adjusted, especially for those assigned to the Covid wards, which included ER. We were divided into three groups with seven days straight duty and then fourteen days off. Some were designated as safety officers to ensure the proper use of PPE. Some office personnel were forced to work from home, especially those older than sixty. The administration continually asked for support from the Office of the President Department of Health and Non-Government Organization.

The government declared Community Quarantine in those affected areas in which Manila is included. Philippine General Hospital (PGH) became one of the Covid referral hospitals. Advisory notices were posted to inform the public about the present set-up at PGH. Transportation was also seized by the government, and most of the employees without private cars had difficulty travelling to the hospital due to the lack of public transport. One of the good things was that many hotels and schools accommodated healthcare workers without charge. In addition, the hospital administration was able to arrange free transportation for employees. On the other hand, healthcare workers were advised to stay in the hotels provided after duty rather than go home, in order to prevent the virus spreading to family members.

Setting up a suitable Covid area was not easy because we also continued to cater for emergency cases. Those that needed to be resuscitated, had trauma, were poisoned, or suffered brain attack seizures, for example, still went to ER. For several months, these numbers had been rising, as had mortality rates. As in other countries, many healthcare workers caught the virus and many did not recover. Some of them were my friends… It was devastating to the health community, but we all needed to be strong.

We still needed to go on duty even if we felt depressed. We also felt afraid, anxious, and angry but kept ourselves composed and didn't lose hope that the pandemic would end. Apart from all the adjustments, the most difficult part of being one of the so-called "Frontliners" was witnessing Covid patients at their worst. Seeing them suffer and eventually die broke our hearts. Added to that was the agony we shared with their relatives who could not say their last goodbyes…

But God is so good and we were able to survive each day because He provided us with all that we needed through the kind-hearted donors from all over the world. We were given enough supplies of PPE, equipment, and food (for patients, their relatives, and employees). Then came the availability of the vaccines (Sinovac and AstraZeneca). Most of the health workers from PGH received the vaccine in the hope that this would help lessen or even eliminate the virus and end this horrible pandemic. A lot had mild to moderate adverse reactions from the vaccine, but all recovered.

As of now, there is a decrease in the number of Covid cases admitted to ER: an average of one or two per day and all of them have mild to moderate symptoms. We are still looking forward to the time when things go back to normal and face masks and shields are not part of our outfit of the day. We continue to pray for God's protection so that we may continue to take care of the sick, especially the underprivileged.

Nurse's experience

Nurse practitioner in a GP practice, West London

During February 2020 we were first made aware of the existence of Covid in the news and media. (It started earlier than this, at the end of December 2019.) Back then, nobody could ever imagine what a devastating impact it would have on all of us. In March 2020 I had visited my family and friends in my hometown, Sheffield, and it was becoming more apparent that we would be facing "lockdown". Still, no one really knew or realised the consequences it would have.

I am currently working as a part-time practice nurse in West London and, by this time, my colleagues and I were starting to feel concerned as we felt that the virus was not being taken seriously. No real measures seemed to have been implemented. Unnecessary, non-urgent appointments were still being booked in, much to the annoyance and frustration of the clinical team. Eventually, we received guidance from the North-West London CCG (Clinical Commissioning Group) which stated that we should only be seeing patients with urgent appointments, routine baby vaccinations, wound care, and warfarin patients. Cervical screening was ceased for a period and chronic disease management, such as diabetic reviews, hypertension, asthma, chronic obstructive airway disease, was conducted over the telephone.

Protective measures started to be implemented: the practice was provided with PPE and hand sanitiser gel. Additionally, deep cleaning was carried out in all the clinical rooms. The chairs were spread out in the waiting rooms and patients were asked to wear a face covering when entering the building. Patients were also advised to book telephone appointments with their GP and renew their prescriptions online. If this was deemed too difficult (especially for the elderly patients) they could post their repeat scripts in a box which was situated in the building. Extended appointments were given with five-minute intervals, which enabled us to clean the working environment. It stopped too many patients being in the surgery.

We continued to work throughout the pandemic over the next few months. It was sometimes stressful and challenging but we managed to provide essential, urgent appointments to our patients. The flu clinic went ahead in September 2020, and we were given longer appointments for each patient which seemed to work well.

The Covid clinics started at our practice in January 2021. We completed our online Covid training and were given additional support prior to each clinic. I found them initially stressful and tiring but the feedback we received from patients was overwhelmingly positive. It felt so good to be part of the vaccination programme team.

Unfortunately, I did catch Covid and felt ill for three weeks. However, I made a speedy recovery and was able to return to work. I was one of the lucky healthcare professionals to survive. Since then, I have had two successful vaccinations that helped protect me in performing my role.

I feel working as a practice nurse in London during the pandemic has been a valuable and unforgettable experience. It has taught me and my colleagues resilience, determination, and courage, even in challenging times. I am very proud of myself and my colleagues. I feel happy and privileged to have helped so many patients.

Nurse's experience

My Story: I work at CHI-St. Luke's The Woodlands, ER, Texas USA

Covid first wave

I remember the first wave of Covid. It was a steep learning curve for me and the rest of my team of healthcare professionals. Every day, we were faced with patients' challenging experiences brought on by the extraordinary nature of the virus. The most unforgettable experience was putting on my PPE for the first time and suffering five seconds of suffocation before I started the fan of my suit! A terrible feeling; in addition, I could not hear much in my suit.

Seeing us in our extraordinary and scary PPE seems to have added to the already terrifying experience of patients as they come into ER. Moreover, I was afraid too as I entered the room with my consultant to treat the patients. Despite the treatment they received, I suspect that they would rather not be in hospital for fear of dying from possible transmission of the virus.

Second wave

After the lockdown, hospitals in our area suffered financially as many either lost staff permanently or were about to lose them. All the necessary Covid protocols and supplies were in place, but no patients came for treatment. One day, however, the floodgates opened and patients returned. Admitting hundreds of patients every day put a lot of pressure on the hospital. PPE supplies ran out and we were issued N95 masks instead, which I was not happy about, but we had no choice.

However, the correct PPE supplies soon arrived and were distributed to all healthcare workers in the hospital. As caregivers, we had to protect ourselves and our families while providing the best possible clinical care to our patients. We would not be able to help others if we were ill ourselves. Before the PPE arrived I was very worried about catching the virus and infecting other family members.

These were extremely difficult times for everyone. All I desired was to be kept safe while performing our duties. We did not have any choice, but I wish I had been able to refuse and say no. Every time I clocked in for work and had my temperature checked, I would drop by our chapel and say a little prayer: "Our Father please bless me Lord and Give me strength. Give me the heart to be part of your healing ministry and give hope to my patients. With this I pray in Jesus' name, Amen."

I decided not to put myself under more pressure by working extra shifts. This decision helped me reduce the risk of catching the virus. In addition, working during the pandemic was very stressful so I just decided to spend my days off relaxing in order to be ready for my next shift. This helped me perform my nursing duties more efficiently as I was more focused and I made fewer mistakes. It is extremely important to be mentally and physically prepared when on duty because every mistake could potentially cause irreversible damage. It is the nurse's duty to preserve as many lives as possible.

I would never have imagined this unprecedented crisis happening during my lifetime, but, despite the difficulties, we managed to cope as a team. I am happy to say I was lucky enough not to catch the virus. Many patients in ER received treatment, recovered, and were discharged and able to tell the story of their miraculous experience. Some, however, were not so lucky, despite our best efforts to save them.

Third wave

Although the wait was long, vaccines were finally approved, distributed, and administered around the globe, including to our hospital. These potentially life-changing discoveries have given hope to everyone that the pandemic can be stopped.

The vaccine roll-out improved the lives for everyone as normality began to return. Restrictions were lifted allowing businesses to open up again. However, a new variant of the virus has evolved, and, as I write, patients, many unvaccinated, are once again flooding into ER. There is still much negativity surrounding vaccination which is making the provision of healthcare challenging. My final message is that people should get vaccinated in order that we can eradicate the pandemic. Vaccinations are safe and effective and they save lives. I hope and pray that one day this pandemic will end so we can all return to our normal lives.

Conclusion

My journey has been painful and excruciatingly difficult since I arrived in the UK. I have faced considerable adversities that pushed me to the limits of my capacity to handle them. I would not have wished this on anyone as it has had a considerable impact on my health. But I would encourage everyone to have the courage to speak out as the more people who do so, the better it will be for society. I am extremely thankful to all my friends, family, and God for guiding me through life. I would not have survived without their support.

I have told my story in order to learn from it and to strengthen me and others. However, I have come to realise that society is dirty with many people intent on committing evil for the sake of power, money, authority, and pride. Many leaders further their careers by covering up the truth and carrying out other wicked deeds.

The journey was an eye-opener for me as I realised some people would sacrifice loyalty and friendship for power and money. Institutions are powerful and they can abuse this power to persecute individuals and by covering up their mistakes. The whole system is corrupt, even lawyers. This applies to unions too. It is their job to protect the employee rather than themselves. But we are living in a society that hungers for and abuses power. This is dangerous as it will only lead to despair and failure. They may succeed in the short term but they will be finally judged in the eyes of God.

My advice is to stay strong, speak out, and stand up for your rights. If you don't do it, no one will. If this doesn't change, our world will continue to get worse by the day. It is just a matter of time before people realise the damage caused by their own failures.

We should always remain positive as, at the end of the day, I believe that things happen for a reason. At the moment, however, I do not know the reason for the adversities I have endured or what they meant, other than that I had to speak out. But they did make me realise how the real world and the organisations within it operate. It seems unfair and immoral that evil triumphed over good and that evil people have been rewarded for their wrongdoings.

In summary, God has given me a great life and all the things I desired such as my beautiful family and home in the UK. Although I have suffered adversities, the experience has made me stronger and more resilient. Having survived these adversities, I now know that I can face whatever circumstances are thrown up at me.

Acknowledgements

I would like to thank my kind and loving husband Alwyn Orr and my children Claire and John Orr for their unfailing love and support throughout writing this book. An additional thank you to Claire for allowing me to use her amazing variety of sketches of the architectural buildings in London.

In addition, my parents Clarita and Lamberto Nunez for the remarkable support they bestowed on me and my siblings, as evidenced by this book.

The Orr family — Robert, Kay, Alison, John, and Michael Mcmullan — who have continually supported me throughout my journey in the UK, especially in my difficult times.

My ancestral family of Buco, Nunez, Pascual, Edwin Mudlong and Padigdig have all given me the strength to carry on while undergoing adversities in my life. I am most thankful.

Special thanks to Auntie Norberta Pascual Mallari who has supported and persuaded me to embark on this remarkable writing adventure that I would never have believed possible.

My Chinese General College nursing friends and teachers, especially Armie Nunez, Raquel Enriquez, Imelda Vecino, Cecille Asistio, Frederick Maglaya, and Irwin Dimaano, who gave constant support and provided and helped shape all the information necessary to complete this book. You are all utterly amazing friends.

For those friends who provided pictures for my book, like Cynthia Lee and Maria Amabelle Valeza Cuerdo. Thank you so much, as my book would not have been completed without your assistance.

My church and family at St Edmunds the King, Northwood and all the Christians who were working behind the scenes, who have given unfailing support and guidance in the way of Christ throughout my journey in the UK, especially for Bernadette Udanton, Jenny Jones, Sarah Parnaby, Marjorie Pimm, Margaret Forsyth, Steve Castle, Father Michael, Carol Diggins, Amanda Roberts, Joyce and Isaac Odeyemi, and Helen Samuel.

My solicitor, Amina Deane, my GP, counsellors, the Royal Free Hospital, Watford Renal Unit, live donation team, and the Imperial team who were part of my journey, notwithstanding how difficult it has been for us.

My next-door neighbour and friend Jennifer Laird who encouraged me to write and start this book. Without you, it would have been impossible to continue. In addition, the support of the Durley Avenue WhatsApp group, especially Veronica.

My UK friends and editor David Gillott, especially Marsha Geyrozaga, Sheryl Tripolli, Lailanee Legaspi, Sally Higgins, Lucy Lardner, Karen Pike, Ema Cammidge, Nor Nori Latip, Yen, Cecille Gubatanga, Cindy Rumingan, Mike and Gill Walters, and Susanna Monge, who provided me with encouragement and support throughout my life in the UK. You have been truly remarkable friends, for better or worse.

I am grateful to my live donation patients who have continually supported me, and to Claire Vaizey Moore and Sharmini Byrne who wrote a story for me about their journey as a donor.

My young, talented, and inspiring beauty queens, Miss Philippines UK Keisha Quijano and Claire Orr, who both contributed stories of their journey to success.

This book would not be complete without the stories of the wonderful nurses regarding their Covid experiences. These were Peejay Padigdig, Marites Obtinario, 'Daisy', Practice Nurse and Percival Rodriquez.

And lastly, to Marie Batey, one of the senior nurses at Imperial Healthcare NHS Trusts, who gave me the opportunity to reflect and who gave me the idea that I could tell the story of my life.

My Next book

Journey through Adversities

Life and adventure from a far distant place in the small village of Baluga

Once upon a time in a small village in the Philippines there lived a couple named Loreta and Gonzalo Nunez, Numerciana and Ambrosio Buco, and their parents and relatives. Here is where their adventures began through love, pain, sorrow, and despair in their fight to survive.

It was not an easy journey as they were part of the generations that lived before and after World War Two, but, at the end of the day, they all managed to pull through. What were the secrets of their success and perseverance? How did they manage to remain positive during this time? This amazing story will thrill us, all the way from their early love life to starting their family, despite their adversities.

Watch out and see!!

The Cheeky Butterfly

Once upon a time there was a family of five butterflies that lived in the foothills of the great mountain of Shera. The three young butterflies always loved playing in their meadow of lush flowers, and it seemed that nothing else mattered in the world other than their endless games. However, one day, one of their lives will change forever, following an event that led him through unforgettable adventures. Will he endure the challenges that come his way? Will he thrive and survive on his quest?

Watch out and see!!

About the Author

My name is Honeylet Nunez Orr. I am a wife and mother of two adorable children. I was born in the Philippines in 1976 and grew up in the small village of Baluga, Talavera, Nueva Ecija. I grew up having a simple, fun, and adventurous lifestyle surrounded by my loving friends and families.

My journey in life through adversities started in the village attending primary school at Homestead 1, through the secondary school at the College of the Immaculate Conception, Cabanatuan City, and then to the Far Eastern University and Chinese General Hospital College of Nursing in Manila.

I graduated with a Bachelor of Science in Nursing in 1997, and initially started working as a private nurse. I then moved to the General Malvar Foundation Hospital, and then the Chinese General Hospital where I stayed for three years before embarking on the next journey of my life in the UK.

I was inspired to write this book as I was passionate to share the journey of my life with others. I wanted to inspire and teach them how perseverance, hard work, and faith can see us through adversities, and that there was light at the end of the tunnel in my life's journey in the Philippines and UK.

You can find me as Honeylet Nunez Orr on social networks, Facebook and Instagram.

Printed in Great Britain
by Amazon